ICE AND FIRE

Ice
&
Fire

DISPATCHES
FROM THE
NEW WORLD
1988-1998

Stephen Osborne

A GEIST BOOK
ARSENAL PULP PRESS
Vancouver

ICE AND FIRE
Copyright © 1998 Stephen Osborne

ARSENAL PULP PRESS
103-1014 Homer Street
Vancouver, BC
Canada v6b 2w9
www.arsenalpulp.com

"Song for Canute" copyright © estate of Jon Furberg
"A Literary Education" copyright © estate of D.M. Fraser

Edited by Mary Schendlinger
Typeset by the Vancouver Desktop Publishing Centre
Printed and bound in Canada

CANADIAN CATALOGUING IN PUBLICATION DATA:
Osborne, Stephen, 1947-

Ice and fire

ISBN 1-55152-061-3

1. Osborne, Stephen, 1947- —Journeys—Canada.
2. Canada—Description and travel. I. Title.
FC75.082 1998   917.104'648   c98-910876-7
F1017.082 1998

The publisher gratefully acknowledges the support of the Canada Council for the Arts for its publishing program, as well as the support of the Book Publishing Industry Development Program, and the B.C. Arts Council.

In remembrance:
D.M. Fraser
1946-1985

CONTENTS

AUTHOR'S NOTE

During the writing of this book I came to understand the New World to be an imaginary place more forgotten than remembered, inhabited nevertheless by real people occupying real landscapes. My first glimpse of the New World was given to me by Daniel Francis in a conversation that began in Ottawa many years ago and continues today. Norbert Ruebsaat led me to consider the constant remaking of the New World by the immigrant generations, and Randy Fred and Lucy Etooangat led me to consider its constant unmaking by successive generations of Native people.

The oldest story in this book is "Nostrum," which I finished in the spring of 1988, when the New World was not quite 496 years old. I am much indebted to Mary Beth Knechtel and Claudia Casper for the encouragement and guidance they gave me as I struggled to find a voice in which to tell that story, and to Viola Fraser, whose kindness to me in New Glasgow allowed me to begin writing it. The most recent of these stories is "Lawn Vité," written ten years later, and for which I owe thanks to Josie Cook, who gave me Bohemian Green Earth, among many other valuable things.

All of the stories in this book are true in the ordinary sense of that word, but how truthfully they are told is for others to judge. Many of them found their present shape after long talks into the night with Laurie Edwards on Gabriola Island and with Tom Walmsley in Toronto. Long talks into the night have much to do with all of these stories, and I am grateful to all of my interlocutors over the years, who include, along with those named above, Roger Dunsmore, Howard White, Bryan Carson, Susan Crean, my brother Tom Osborne, Quita Francis, Linda Field, and some who are no longer in this world: Jon Furberg, Brian Shein, Greg Enright, Shotaro Iida and D. M. Fraser.

I wish also to acknowledge my parents, Wanda and Jim Osborne, whose love and support have made many things possible, and whose stories, which I am only beginning to learn, have become the subject of so much that remains to be told.

Most of these stories were published (some in much different form) in *Geist* magazine, and I am grateful to the Geist Foundation (especially Barbara Zatyko, Dennis Priebe and my sister Patty Osborne) for keeping that publication alive and for allowing me space in it. In putting these stories into a book I have discovered again what a pleasure it is to have Brian Lam as publisher and friend and I thank him for his tremendous patience over a protracted period of revision and extended deadlines.

This book could not have been written without the implied consent of those who appear in it and I hope that by putting these stories into the world I am giving back something of what has been given to me. Someone who appears by name in only one of these stories is in fact present in all of them: she is Mary Schendlinger, whose fine editorial hand has led me again and again out of the tangle of syntactical underbrush in which I so often find myself; hers was the first ear to detect what might be valuable here, and I will be forever grateful for the understanding that she has brought into my life. This book owes whatever strengths it has to her fearless attentions; what weaknesses remain are proof only of how much more I have to learn.

—S.O.

Vancouver

11 November 1998

LOOKING FOR COLUMBUS

ARUBA

Five months after his seventy-fourth birthday my father went off for two weeks of windsurfing on an island named Aruba, which he told me later is one of the few places in the Caribbean that makes no claim to having been the landfall made by Columbus in 1492. Aruba is a true desert island with cactuses growing on it and no trees or hills to impede the trade winds that blow continuously over it. While my father was telling me this, I remembered reading an essay a few days earlier about Edmund Gosse, the English intellectual who disgraced himself by claiming that cactuses grew in the desert into which Moses led his people, when it had been known for three centuries that cactuses are not found in the Old World. Off the lee shore of Aruba the sea is flat and the wind is strong: these are ideal conditions for windsurfing, my father said, as long as you don't get blown out to sea by the offshore breeze. A further advantage to the Aruban lee shore is the shallowness of the ocean there, as I remember him putting it, a shallowness which continues for a great distance, so that if you fall off the board you have only to stand up in the water to avoid drowning. This was a relief to me, although only in a retrospective way, since during the time of my father's absence I had been under the misapprehension that he was risking his life windsurfing in the mouth of the Columbia River, which I imagined to be a place of rough seas, treacherous currents and vicious crosswinds. The only inconvenience encountered by my father on what I think of now as the Calm Aruban Sea was the sudden acceleration that occurred when the sailboard, with the wind in the right quarter, stepped up onto the flat surface and began to plane over the sea, an effect which he said could be "rather terrifying at times." The harness provided with the board was designed to help you withstand sudden accelera tion, but if you happened to shift your weight in a certain way while moving at speed, it tended to fling you into the air in the manner of a slingshot. The result could be a broken or cracked rib, said my father, and he put his hand to his side, where he was pretty sure that one of his ribs had a crack in it. He had seen no evidence of deep poverty on Aruba, he went on to say, although he had been made uneasy by the sight of tourist buses disgorging senior citizens into the casinos at ten o'clock in the morning. The drinking water in Aruba was the best he had ever tasted, and he was surprised to learn that its source was a desalination plant, where seawater was rendered palatable by a process that neither of us understood very well. Later I looked again into the essay about Edmund Gosse and found no reference to the mistake about the cactus that I remembered so clearly to have been there. Edmund Gosse had been mistaken about many things, but cactus in the Old World was apparently not one of them.

TERRA NOVA

Within minutes of leaving the airport at St. John's, I began to suspect that my fingernails were growing more rapidly. We had been losing time all day, pressing eastward five thousand miles against the sun. "There's a hundred and sixty bars in this town," the cabbie said without moving his lips. He pronounced it *honerdnsixty-baihrs*, in a musical voice not easily rendered in conventional orthography: "Ats mordenwhan pertousan you know, percapita." We began going into the bars as soon as we could, to perch on stools and lean our elbows on the dark polished wood. The Guinness came slowly from the pump, black and thick with a creamy head that clung to the glass all the way down. From time to time I could feel a quickening in my fingertips, a brief vertiginous tingle beneath the horny carapace.

We were in a city made of wood: clapboard sidings painted in bright pastels, interiors varnished and lighted by incandescent tungsten—a Popeye the Sailor Man town: narrow streets layered into the cliffside and yoked together on the longitude by steep stone stairways. We mounted a crumbling flight of stairs to the next level, and another street opened before us like a page in a children's pop-up book, low bar fronts and house doors leaning into the pavement, elegant in their ramshacklery, lacking all quaintness.

We paused to take breath, and to peer up and down. And to feel our bodies, which seemed mysteriously to have enlarged themselves, adjusting to the scale of this atavistic wooden city. The air was cold, permeated by the bleak Atlantic; the sky was leaden grey; we found the cheerless prospect secretly exhilarating. Down by the harbour an improvised signboard made of white plastic and movable black letters proclaimed this to be the oldest city on the continent. The continent is considered to be attached to this place, we supposed, despite the body of ocean we overflew so long ago. There is almost no evidence of historicity in this ancient place: up the hill a massive stone cathedral, its ramparts streaked with fungus, looks out over the harbour toward a solitary stone tower on a bald hillside on the opposite shore. "That's John Cabot's tower," said the waiter in a bar near the shore, "or maybe Marconi's house—one or the other, that's sure." We too were unconcerned.

Late Saturday night hotdog vendors appeared on street corners, their portable ovens making warm places in the gritty blowing snow. At one of them we tendered small change to a short smiling man who was rocking up and down on his toes to keep warm. He was cheerful but we, briefly, were not: why must he sell hotdogs in the middle of the night? No one asks. Earlier in the day we had eaten a meal of cod's tongues and scrunchions and paid seventeen percent in sales tax. In the Duke of Duckworth tavern three men and a woman began to sing Irish songs and to perform Irish tunes on guitar, bass, hand-held drum, flute, mandolin, banjo and squeezebox, filling the room with a rolling cacophony that swept all before it. The performers were young, and when they ran out of songs they began again at the beginning and kept on singing long into the night. Standing at the urinal in this most straightforward of cities, I asked the strangers beside me if any of them might know the whereabouts of a friend who had moved here years ago; within minutes I was on the phone behind the bar talking to my friend.

Back into the street, the alley, the rocky stairs, into the swirl of glittering snow already ankle-deep on the ground. A huge wind walloping up the hill: we pushed along and up through the whistling silence, past the sleeping flat-faced houses brunting the sidewalk. Now the air was filled with a generous cold that stung our foreheads as if to caution us. Next day, some miles east at the iceberg-viewing point, we could taste the appropriate rolling fog as wind and snow and hard rain battered the easternmost edge of the continent. We dispersed along the shingle to peer out to sea, into the swirling miasma, toward the iceberg that we had been told was there to be seen. Back in the city a notice in the museum told us that 25,000 vessels lie wrecked in a sunken ring around this land.

When it was time to go we hailed a cab, and on the way to the airport I discovered that my fingernails had grown out past my fingertips. The cabbie tossed me his clippers in a straightforward way and I began gratefully to carve away. "Let it fall on the floor," said the cabbie, as he fishtailed the cab out onto the icy highway. "Believe me sore, I seen a lotta things. This is a dreadful place for drivin'." Later, at 30,000 feet, I remembered two things: one, attached to a grocery store on the edge of the wooden city, a sign reading Live Bait and Barbecue Sauce; the other, a resonant, strangely appropriate epigram at the head of a page of *Hints On Sea Risks*, a book published in 1844 on display in the museum: "Even a sober landsman is more useful than a drunken sailor."

LOOKING FOR COLUMBUS

News of the Columbus statue reached me in 1993, in February, through a friend who had been told that a monument to the Admiral of the Ocean Sea could be found in Vancouver somewhere along the lower reaches of Clark Drive, near the elevated railway. I set out to find it in the morning in my Toyota, and within minutes I was steaming down Clark Drive, which is the main truck route into the city, fighting for position in a torrent of eighteen-wheelers and huge flatbeds loaded down with heavy machinery. I swept several times up and down Clark Drive but saw no sign of a statue anywhere along the way, and I began to doubt the news that my friend, who held a post-graduate degree in communications theory, had passed on to me from his unnamed informant. I drove into the neighbouring streets, and after questioning two elderly gents in fedoras who claimed to know nothing of a statue of Columbus, I hailed a teenaged boy who said that he knew where a statue was to be seen, just around the corner and across the street on Clark Drive, one block away. Was it Columbus, I asked. He had no idea. I returned to Clark and in minutes found what I had been seeking, hidden within a circular hedge of concrete slabs set into the ground directly beneath the elevated railway. I left the car in the parking lot of an adjacent auto body shop and walked out onto the sidewalk and into the enclosure, and there for the first time beheld the statue of Christopher Columbus that I had not known to be there until moments ago.

The statue sat on the top of a concrete plinth about eight feet high. It was a bronze figure of a prepubescent boy perched at the edge of a wharf; he was wearing leggings and pointy shoes and his long hair trailed past his shoulders from beneath a soft cloth cap. His legs were crossed at the knee and he held a book in his lap, from which he appeared to have turned away in order to peer down into the implied waters of an imaginary sea. I had to stand in that sea in order to look up into his eyes, which were blank but compelling nevertheless. The enclosure in which he reposed had been shaped into a tiny amphitheatre above which the heavy mass of the overhead railway swept out toward the distant reaches of the city. The three tiers of the amphitheatre were covered in grime. A plaque beneath the statue confirmed it to be Christopher Columbus, "donated by the Citizens of Genoa, Supported by the Region of Liguria, Erected by the Confratellanza Italo-Canadese," and dedicated to the memory of a deceased jurist of Italian ancestry. Another much smaller plaque bore only a date: 11 October 1986, which I took to be the date of its dedication. I imagined people gathering here for the unveiling, the cutting of a ribbon perhaps; a speech certainly must have been made, and the air must have been heavy (as it was now) with exhaust fumes and the roar of diesel engines and the crash of air brakes, and the squeal of the commuter train passing overhead. This was an unlikely site for a monument, hidden along a truck route, surrounded by low warehouse buildings, premises of the Dry Ice and Gases (Western) Ltd., Pacific Ice Co. Inc., and the anagrammatically named Adanac Carpet Ltd. In the south I could read the hand-painted signboards of Jesse's Moving and Storage, and half a block north the massive plastic signage of the Helping Prevent Child Abuse Thrift Store, another long low warehouse in a neighbourhood of long low warehouses. It was a site made for camouflage and not for display, and this elaborate assemblage of bronze boy and plinth, amphitheatre and walled enclosure seemed to have been put here in order to be forgotten, not remembered.

Christopher Columbus is rarely celebrated in this country, which prefers to claim discovery by the other Genoese, Juan Caboto, who, as John Cabot, sank into the waters of the North Atlantic after boasting in 1497 in the streets of Bristol that he had discovered the lost Island of the Seven Cities, a place never seen again by human eyes. The monument on Clark Drive is possibly the only memorial in the country dedicated to Christopher Columbus, Admiral of the Ocean Sea, Viceroy and Governor General, in the words of the charter signed by the king of Spain, "of all lands that he might find on his journey to China." Whatever else might be said of him, Columbus was a better sailor than Cabot; during his successful eight crossings of the Atlantic, his observations of star, wind and current led him to conclude that the earth was shaped like a pear, its upper protuberance a great swelling in the ocean sea near the equator, at the summit of which lay the earthly paradise, site of the Tree of Life and source of the four great rivers found in Scripture. No one remembers Columbus for that now.

A few months ago I returned to the Columbus monument, which I had not visited for five years, on foot this time, by way of the Helping Prevent Child Abuse Thrift Store where I picked up a copy of *Swamp Angel* for fifty cents. The statue of the dreaming boy was still on its plinth, and I had forgotten how beautiful it was. The amphitheatre was still covered in grime and the thunder of the traffic streaming by was unceasing. The site remained as it had been, a place of desolation, and nothing seemed to have changed during my absence. Then I saw that the plaque with the dedication on it had been taken away; four holes drilled in the face of the concrete marked where it had been; and then I understood that everything had changed.

For who now besides me (and a handful of anonymous dignitaries) would know that this bronze boy was Christopher Columbus? All that remained to identify him were the day and the year engraved on the smaller plaque, which had been left untouched, and which I studied for a moment before realizing that the day inscribed there, 11 October, was my mother's birthday. When next I saw my mother I mentioned this to her and she said it was no coincidence; she had known since going to New York City on her birthday years ago that this was the day Columbus discovered America, an event which in New York City was celebrated by a parade. Later I looked into Morisson's biography of Columbus and read that the distant light which Columbus claimed to see on October 11, a Thursday, at ten o'clock at night, no one else saw; it was not until the next day at two o'clock in the morning that one of his crewmen saw the distant shadow of the land that lay before them. The light that Columbus saw on my mother's birthday, the eleventh of October, was the light of his own obsession, and the people who embraced him on the shore of Guanahani on the twelfth of October would be extinguished by that light. Perhaps this is what we are to remember today in the now unnamed monument hidden away under the elevated railway on Clark Drive.

ANATOL

Anatol was eighty-four years old when he broke his neck in Regina by falling down as he was getting out of his chair in the living room, and then he got up off the floor and sat down again. The next day he felt a pain in the back of his head and his wife took him to the hospital, where he remained sixteen days, having broken c2 and c3, which are the vertebrae alongside the brain stem, as his wife Gillian put it when she told me this story a couple of months after it happened. We were in her car and she was driving slowly through the hushed streets of Regina toward the condominium in which she lived with Anatol on the edge of the city, where the snow on the streets had not yet been scraped away. It was early evening and the city lay everywhere muffled in winter twilight. The doctors had to put Anatol into a halo in order to keep his neck straight, said Gillian. A halo is a metal band that screws into the skull, and when I shook hands with Anatol a few minutes later I could see two little dents in his forehead where the screws had gone in.

Anatol was tall and thin and somewhat shaky after the accident but he carried himself with a dignified air that seemed to raise the tone ever so slightly; he poured out perfect martinis and sat in his chair and I sat on the sofa opposite him while Gillian finished preparing the dinner that he had begun in the kitchen nook. It was cozy in the condominium, and we drank the martinis very slowly as Anatol described the accident that Gillian had told me about and that had humiliated him when it happened. I was much aware of being a long way from home in a city that I did not know, and then Anatol said that he could remember clearly the day in Vienna when the First World War began.

It was the day Archduke Ferdinand was assassinated in Sarajevo. They were eating dinner, the whole family together—by dinner, Anatol said, he meant the midday meal—when the nurse came in with his little sister, who was then less than a year old, and who was now almost seventy-eight years old. The nurse was out of breath and very pale. "They've shot the Archduke," she said. There was a very tense feeling in the air. A little bit later the phone rang and it was the War Department—Anatol's family had one of the few telephones in the city at that time because his father was a senior official in the department—and his father had to go over there right away. That afternoon he took Anatol and his brother for a walk over to the old emperor's castle, where there was a gloom in the air—no, said Anatol, what is the word?—a despondency—and there were hundreds of people all walking over to the castle and crowding around. They wanted to know what the old emperor was going to do. But the emperor was probably very happy; everyone knew that he hated the Archduke, who was his nephew.

The prime minister at that time was known as the emperor prime minister, because he ruled by decree. He was a count, and he always ate lunch in a restaurant near the castle. He was eating there one day after the war started when a man came up to him and said, Mister prime minister? The count looked up and the man aimed a pistol at him. Bang bang, he said, you are dead. And he shot the emperor prime minister in the head.

It was a political murder, said Anatol; the man who did it did it for representative government, because there was none of that then. Anatol's father took the boys over to the War Department and a friend of his father's said, Look, maybe the boys would like to see the body of the prime minister. So they went into another room and there he was, the dead prime minister, laid out with flowers everywhere, wearing a black suit. There was a hole in his forehead and another on one side of his head. Anatol was greatly impressed by the dead prime minister and said that it had made a very large impression on him.

The last time Anatol saw the old emperor, Franz Josef, was in 1916. The Austrian army, with the Germans, had had an important victory, although the Austrians were really finished by that time. Anatol remembered being with his mother in the train station shortly before the battle, and there was a German officer on the platform. Anatol's mother asked him where he was going, and the officer said—I want to get it right, the exact expression, said Anatol. The officer said: we are going to pull the cart out of the shit.

So the Germans saved the day, and it was a big day in Vienna. Anatol's parents took the family over to the castle, and there were thousands of people there, maybe two hundred thousand. There was nowhere for them to get a view, but then Anatol's mother saw a policeman who was a cousin of hers and he got them up onto a nearby roof, where they sat next to the wife of the mayor. Eventually the old emperor came out on the balcony to salute the people. He waved his hand. He was wearing his uniform, as he always did, and there were stars hanging from it along with the Golden Fleece, which was tucked up under his neck. Two months later the old emperor was dead.

In 1918, before the war had ended, Anatol's father took him out of the classical school and put him in the military school, which he could do at no cost to himself because of his position in the War Department. Now there would be one fewer mouth to feed at home. The food at the military school was terrible. There was a dessert every night that seemed to Anatol to be nothing but garden worms and he couldn't bear to eat it. He persuaded another boy to trade him his bread ration for it; the bread was musty and rank but it wasn't as bad as the worms.

As things got worse there was sickness in the school, and boys died, and some of them were Anatol's classmates. He went with his classmates to see one of his dead friends, and that was when he smelled the terrible stench of death, which he said was unbearable. It made him think of the taste of the musty bread that he was trading the wormy dessert for. After that he couldn't eat the bread either, because of the smell of the dead boy.

But he must have eaten something that winter, as he said at the end of the story, because he survived.

FAMILY ALBUM

When my parents lived on Baffin Island in the late forties, they took many photographs with a fixed-focus Kodak and developed the film in the hospital darkroom. They made prints in a contact frame exposed to the light of the Coleman lantern in their living room. About two hundred of these two- by three-inch photographs survive, held down onto heavy black pages by little die-cut gummed and folded corners. A fancy cord once bound the pages together between heavy leather boards. Eventually a shoelace replaced the cord and today even the shoelace is gone. But the leather boards are still there, and the album remains intact in an outsize manila envelope.

The photographs my parents took are formally much like the snapshots one finds in any family album of the period. Captions hand-lettered in white ink provide a coy commentary to images of family, friends and neighbourhood. But it is precisely this subject matter that sets the album apart from most others like it. In one of the pictures, captioned "Man with Whip," a man in fur parka and leggings is handling the long whip. His face is almost hidden and so small as to be nearly unrecognizable. He has turned his face toward the camera as if he might be wary of catching the back of his head with the whip end. One foot is moving, and he appears to be leaning both into and out of the big blurred arc of the whip which has just passed his head: its contour snakes down along the snow and trails faintly past the framing edge. There are no dogs in the picture; the man is demonstrating for the camera. As a boy I often looked at this picture, and today I have it in my desk drawer. The man with the whip is clearly my father—with a magnifying glass I can make out his features—but the clothes he wears and the position of his body belong to another world. In a landscape of white and grey he cracks a long whip. This image is as strange and exciting to me now as it was when I was five years old in Edmonton, learning to recognize images of the place where I was born.

In another photograph, more artfully composed, a man stands on a komatik. He too wears parka and leggings and he holds a telescope up to one eye. The telescope rests on an upright harpoon, a lens cap dangling from one end. The picture was taken from low down, so that man, komatik, harpoon and telescope make an arresting silhouette against a ground of white fog. In my childhood this image was the very emblem of the exotic; it belongs in the gallery of adventure imagery, as my parents must have known when they gave it a caption: "Eetowanga checks the trail."

My parents left Baffin Island when I was two years old and my brother six months. The photo album became the centrepiece of our family iconography—for our sisters, too, who came later. It was an album unlike any of our friends' albums and it went with us, along with many delicate ivories carved by Eetowanga, as we moved from city to city following our father's career. We became familiar with the people in the album and knew their names; we could point them out to our friends. Especially the man with the telescope, Eetowanga, and his family, for it was they who had looked after our family. At the dinner table we heard many stories of the north: how to find, shoot, spear and butcher a seal; how to get the komatik over the reef; how to build a snowhouse; how Eetowanga predicted the weather, interpreted dreams, found substitutes for water. On my father's desk stood a framed portrait of Eetowanga; his face was as familiar as any of our own.

Our parents used the language they had learned in the north to speak privately in front of us, and a few words of Inuktitut crept into the household language: *peeloacto* (too much); *ayunungmut* (oh, what the hell); my boyhood penis was *ooshoo*, a euphonious word that lasted my brother and me until puberty. Our family mythology was made up of images and stories taken not from the lives of our forebears, but from the place of my birth, a black and white place preserved in the family album, forever removed from the mundane world in which we moved. The album was all that was needed to make a past; there was no need to look further back.

As a child dealing with other children, I found a certain advantage in being from such a place, but as I grew older and began to learn something of history, I could sense that my birthplace did not belong to me in the way the photo album did; I could claim the images (or be claimed by them), but I could never claim the place.

When I was thirty-five my father took me back to Pangnirtung. It was June and everything was in full colour twenty-four hours a day, awash in a strange warm light that made objects at a distance stand out in relief. It was like looking through Polaroid sunglasses, or at the paintings of Henri Rousseau. Nothing in the album could have prepared me for the shimmering air of Pangnirtung: I had no words for the particular colours of things, and none for the shapes of the land or the soft green and blue undulations of a melting iceberg that lay stranded in the shallows.

Most of the buildings in the old photographs were still there but they had been appropriated to new uses. The hospital was now a community centre and the women there laughed when they held out their hands to demonstrate how small I had been when they last saw me. Eetowanga, who met us at the plane with many of his family and friends, took us into the room in which I was born and I looked out the window to see what my mother would have seen: a stretch of open ground, a few white buildings, and beyond, the glassy fiord. The doctor's house was still there too, shifted to a new spot, now the office of a local crafts organization. There were many new buildings, of course, but in the old ones scattered among them

I could feel the eerie traces of the family album. After my father went home, I stayed on for a few more weeks. My first day alone, I felt foolish and lost. But the next day Eetowanga appeared and said to me, *atata audlakpok*. Then he worked with gestures until I understood him to say, father goes away. Now I was alone in the place of my birth, which I must learn to see again.

LOST LAND

And a long forgotten
lonely cairn of stones.

—from "Northwest Passage,"
by Stan Rogers

Not long ago in the university library I found a shelf filled
with books that had never been checked out. These were accounts
of early navigators collected in the seventeenth century by Richard
Hakluyt and Samuel Purchas: here were Frobisher, Hudson, Foxe,
James and dozens whose names were unknown to me. I fell into
these books as into a dream, and took them home in a box. Since
then I have been lost at sea repeatedly, in tiny ships that smell of
pitch and tar and the stale beer that sustained their crews. These
were the ancient men whose stories, two hundred years later,
lighted Coleridge to his greatest poem—just as Hudson, who per-
ished in Canadian ice while Shakespeare was writing *The Tempest*,
was said to have lit some many others into an unknown sea.

Then I remembered that once I too had yearned to meet an
ancient mariner, and I wondered how one might dare to imagine
such a man. Perhaps I would say to him: how was it, when you
were there? And he would say: what we saw, you will never see,
nor will I see it again, now. I would get out my pen and begin to
write, and he would say: it was exactly how it was:

First took we ship in June, a Thursday, on the ebb tide and the river gathered us softly down to the estuary; here our Captain made known to us his orders, by which we were to serve God each day in the form of the church established by our sovereign, and card-playing and swearing were to be forsaken, and filthy communication banished forever from among us. We were twelve men and a boy and we filled up the waist of the ship as the Captain prayed over us to Him Who maketh the whirlwind to calm, and hushed are the billows of the deep.

Hence we sailed over the sea until month's end, our Captain holding his course north by west toward that unknown part of the world, so far that we came at last to the place where we found no night at all, but a continual light and brightness of the sun shining clearly upon the huge and mighty sea. Now saw we our first ice, which the man on the foredeck mistook for white swans in the nearness. But the breeze coming down carried into our nostrils a thin perfume like a trace of alum caught in our throats; this our Captain said was the exhalation of the ice mountains that lay against the warm Polar Sea, and soon we began to perceive a distant wall of ice driving toward us in a great heap. Then the wind shifted to southeast by south, and began a great storm that forced us to lie a-hull for half a day before the wind swung abeam and knocked us flat upon the raging surface of the sea. Now the ship filled with water and lay as good as sunk, and the men clung to her awash in the icy main. In this distress, when all the men had lost their courage, our Captain crept along the gunwale as the seas broke over him and he caught onto the foresail by the weather leach; this he grasped in both hands and then he stood upright and leaned heavily away, thereby to help her to her feet. Some among us joined him in this labour and at last she became upright and we put her to spoon before the sea all that day and the next as we worked the pumps a hundred strokes to the hour. In this storm we lost the boy, whose name was Richard Carey, and the barber surgeon, one Thomas Runckel of Norfolk, both taken from their distress by He Who bringeth them out and leadeth men to the haven of their desire. So spake our Captain when the storm abated, and he took their few belongings to his cabin, that they might be later auctioned to those before the mast. Now some among us made known their desire to continue running south until we had run back home again. But this our Captain would not hear, and he bore the tiller fiercely over to bring us round again to northwest by north.

The sea was very much tossed and the wind carrying off the tops of the waves made a kind of rain, in which the rays of the sun painted the colours of a rainbow. And then we saw a strange sight in the element. On each side of the sun there appeared another sun, and two rainbows that passed clean through them and then two rainbows more, the one compassing round the suns and the other crossing through the whole circumference. Here was an emanation beyond our understanding. Our Captain ordered victuals brought up from the hold that we might set out the salt meat to dry and our clothing also; and he set a watch on the foredeck so that we might repair our bodies in sleep under hatches and before the ague began to take hold on us. We proceeded thus before a triple sun, in a damp and miserable half-sleep, as our Captain held our course toward the unknown lands.

In the morning (by the glass, there being no night in those parts), one of the watch, looking overboard, saw a mermaid, and called the company to see her, but only his fellow watchman came up to him; by that time the mermaid was come close to the ship's side, and was looking earnestly upon them. She rolled over in the sea and from the navel upward, her back and breasts were like a woman's (as they say that saw her), her body as big as one of us; her skin was very white; and long hair hanging down behind, of colour black: in her going down they saw her tail, which was like the tail of a porpoise, and speckled like a mackerel. Those who saw her were Thomas Hilles and Robert Rayner, honest men whom our Captain later questioned separately before making affirmation of their truthfulness.

Then came the fog upon us in thin tatters that soon were collected into a loathsome veil that oppressed our vision and made the sun a bloody stain in the element. The sun vanished altogether, and the wind dropped to a small breeze; we could hear a mournful sound far off, which grew into a miserable howling such as the souls of the damned might make, and we knew not what it was, for we could see no farther than a pike's length in any direction. Our Captain bade us stand at the gunwales with oars and pikes and the ice came invisibly upon us, striking our stem a blow that threatened to break the ship's knees; then did several leap unto the ice so as to fend away the ship from devastation. Now began our great labour with the ice, in which we lost Samuel Small who slipped into the sea with a feeble cry and no one able to reach him. It began to fall snow when the fog lifted and we could perceive the sea to be infested by monstrous great islands of ice: some of these were the size of great cathedrals, things rare and wonderful, and greatly to be regarded. For the length of four watches we struggled with rope and axe to find our way among them, and the snow was half a foot deep on the foredeck.

Then came the sun back to us suddenly with such heat that the pitch began to ooze from between the planks. Now saw we our first land in the nearness, and the Captain put the small boat down to pull us into shelter in a tiny harbour surrounded by cliffs of black stone strewn with ice and snow. Against the far shore lay a great mountain of ice of a perfect azure colour like to the sky itself. Here we dropped anchor in ten fathoms and took rest in the burning light of the sun.

In the morning our Captain took with him such as had strength and we entered the unknown land in marching order, with ensign displayed. There knelt we down at his command, and thanked God for our safe arrival and for the long life of the Queen, for whom this country, which our Captain named The Queen Her New Land, he pronounced to be taken in possession, in the hope of salvation in Christ our Redeemer. We marched through the country, and now and then we heaped up stones on hilltops and other places in token of her Majesty's possession, and we picked up stones and moss in handfuls to take with us for proof of our finding. On the west shore we found a dead fish floating, which had in his nose a horn straight and twisted like a screw, of two yards length and broken at the tip, where we perceived it to be hollow; this we carried away as further proof of possession, and some of our sailors later putting spiders within its tip, which presently died, we supposed it by virtue of this test to be the Unicorn of the Sea. Found we no sign of a country people, until the third day when the carpenter, searching for pieces of wood, uncovered a sepulchre of stones, in which lay the bones of several persons. These we examined closely for evidence of cloven feet, for some claim that only devils inhabit unknown lands, but found we no such evidence. Nor found we any living people, that we might honourably return home with them captive.

Now had we a new land, a place of rock and moss, and bones and a single Unicorn's horn. On its northern shore lay a broken waste of ice that lay everywhere beneath the sun and up to the horizon. One quarter of our crew were perished; and who still alive could be certain of seeing home again? Now must our Captain put away his letters to the Kings of China and Japan, and put too his wilfulness aside, lest he offend Him without Whose blessing we would never gain passage to our homes. Sorrowfully then did he put up the helm and we departed this unknown land, which no Christian would ever see again.

Thus would my ancient man pause in his story, were he to survive and see home again.

TURNING THE WHEEL

The man was Japanese and he was wearing what at the time I knew from newspaper photographs to be a white cotton Nehru suit, including the hat. He was carrying a reel-to-reel tape recorder and a wicker stool with a padded leather top. There were two of us waiting in the classroom in Vancouver when he came in late and out of breath. This was many years ago, and although I cannot remember what we said, I am certain that he bowed to us before opening up the machine and setting out the two speakers. His name was Iida, and he said that we might call him Iida-san. The class was Chinese Mahayana Buddhism. I had found it listed in the university calendar and, convinced that it would be oversubscribed (this was 1968), had gone to the campus at six in the morning on registration day. But as it turned out, I was the only registrant for the course, so I persuaded my girlfriend, who was an architecture student, to register as well.

His manner was brusque, although less so when he was older, I think, than then. He moved abruptly and spoke in short bursts: his voice was pitched to another language. Strangers were disconcerted by him. Some stepped back in his presence and assumed a patronizing attitude. Surely he was aware of this. At one time I accounted for it by ascribing it to his difficulty with English. But of course there is more to it than that. Others, on meeting him, were quick to demonstrate a curiosity, or a heightened interest. It is to these interested strangers that he directed his attention and his work.

It soon became clear that he was uneasy with intricate machinery. I threaded the tape into the machine for him and got the wires connected to the box. Later I would have occasion to assist him in the operation of projectors, movie screens and complex locks. He once told me that the only machine he had ever mastered was the one-speed bicycle he rode to work. We sat quietly for a few more minutes, and when we could see that no one else would arrive, he turned on the tape. It was a recording of Mahatma Ghandi chanting sutras.

In citizenship court a couple of years later—my girlfriend and I were his sponsors—he could answer none of the questions about provincial politics. (Tommy Douglas was running at the time in a Nanaimo by-election). He explained his ignorance to the judge by saying that his time was taken up with scholarly reading and the only popular press he had time to read was *Time* magazine, which he read every week. For many years the influence of *Time* magazine was strongly apparent in his English writing style.

We sat for an hour listening to the tape. The language was Sanskrit, and of course it was completely opaque to us. He sat cross-legged on the stool, his head lowered, gesturing from time to time with hand or eye to indicate important or beautiful passages. He seemed to know the words and accompanied them occasionally in a strange, weirdly pitched drone. It was disconcerting but not uncomfortable. I found myself paying attention to the syllables, not one of them familiar, even as sound.

He is the only one of my teachers who became a friend to me. This was directly a result of his willingness to move outside the academic world. When I left the university and became involved in publishing, he simply widened his reach so that my work included his and his mine. He was able to translate himself between the communities of separation within which we all find our consignments. For this he risked ostracism both on the campus and off.

35

He is talking about archery. He turns his head toward the imaginary target and in the same motion opens the imaginary bow between his hands. The effect is of grace, integrity and power. It takes your breath away. I have seen the same liquid motion in his demonstration of Kendo movements, and in putting a stone down on a Go board. The gesture, once begun, is sure, inevitable. But when he enters a room his movements seem erratic, arbitrary.

We are sitting in the bar, half a dozen of us, and Iida is talking to the novelist. He has the novelist's book open in front of him and he is asking the novelist difficult questions. Some of the questions he answers himself. Another night we are joined by the actor who played the school principal in *Who Has Seen the Wind*, which was on television a few nights earlier. Iida recognizes him with a start; he bows and shakes his hand. Teaching during the war, in that small place, he says, that must have been difficult. Well, yes, said the actor, but I'm only an actor, really. Oh, that is nothing, says Iida, you see, you were a very good teacher.

We did not agree on the model of the successful Japanese corporation. What I perceived to be a shadow of the corporate state, he described as a kind of workers' paradise. But he agreed that he would be unable to work under such idyllic conditions

Among the graffiti and printed ephemera that found their way onto our office walls, there once appeared a page torn from a Japanese magazine. It was an advertisement for cameras and showed a laughing child emerging from the ocean. The child was holding up a large crab in one hand and waving toward a man holding a camera. Someone had circled the block of Japanese text at the top of the ad and scribbled in a mock translation: *Don't laugh, you've got 'em too.* Iida studied this notation for some minutes but was baffled by it. Then, when the joke was explained to him, he convulsed with laughter. After that he became a student of "the Canadian joke," as he called it, carefully examining the graffiti on our walls and occasionally bringing new specimens into the office for our assessment. He thought we should compile a Canadian joke book for Japanese tourists. There are no jokes in Japanese, he said, not jokes like these.

In the summers he travelled—with very little money, in those early years. One summer I put him on the train to Ottawa, in a seat in the day coach. He had a small pressboard suitcase and a shopping bag filled with little cellophane packages of dried Ramen noodles. These were his sustenance; all he needed was hot water, which the dining car would provide free. He was intending to raise money in Ottawa to pay for a ticket to Oslo, where a conference of Buddhist scholars would be convening later in the month. I didn't think there would be anyone in Ottawa in July, especially anyone with money to give to a transient professor, but he was serene: this was turning the wheel of dharma, it was right action—and the future would take care of itself. A few weeks later a card arrived in the mail from Oslo.

Turning the wheel of dharma: he used the expression lightly, but it resonated throughout his work. I was a student of literature, so he assigned me the study of Japanese poetry as an introduction to Zen. My girlfriend was a student of art, so she studied painting and calligraphy. These were more than mere assignments; they were the means of collaborating in a larger project: a way of knowing the world. The class grew to five or six, and each participant brought a new discipline to bear on the work. We met with Iida at odd hours throughout the week and occasionally all together in his office, when he would lecture, often beginning with a single word: *void*, for instance, to which he would apply a linguistic analysis back through time, across many languages. He debated with us in the manner of the Tibetan monks: providing antithesis to thesis, turn and turn about.

His triumph was the Asian Studies Centre at the University of B.C., an elegant structure next to the Japanese gardens. It is a story that was painful to him for many years. The year of the Osaka Exposition, he had arranged to spend the summer in India and Nepal. Some days before leaving he met me at the Japanese Gar-

dens and showed me a scrap of paper on which he had scribbled
the dimensions of the nearby parking lot, in paces. He had decided
to stop over in Osaka, he said, where he intended to find a building
that would fit on the lot. When he called me a few months later to
ask me for lunch, I had forgotten all about it. Through the lunch
he spoke only of India and Nepal, and when we finished he went
out to the car with me and got in and said, now I have something
to show you. He directed me out of the campus and into the
university endowment lands to a clearing in the woods, where,
scattered over an acre or so, lay dozens of huge wooden crates with
Russian markings on them. It was the Sanyo building from Osaka,
and it had cost him one dollar.

We used to argue about Mishima's suicide, but neither of us
could provide arguments that worked for the other. At times I
thought him to be merely intransigent. But when I was in the habit
of visiting his classroom once a year, I was always surprised to be
reminded of how direct and open he was in the exchange with his
students. I could see that his seminars embraced an ever-widening
mix of political and cultural currents, and that I forget too easily
that the university is still important, that growth can take place
there.

He was attracted to the baroque and rococo; hence his tendency
toward the Tantric. I, on the other hand, was drawn to the austerity
of Zen. We tended to cross paths there, in the psychedelic sixties:
he was at home at a light show with plenty of music, while I
yearned for the sere air of asceticism. In the eighties I made
criticism of the political implications of both Zen and the Tantra.
He was always ready to engage in dharma combat on these topics.

I never consciously modelled my behaviour on his. But his
commentary was inclusive of the world we live in and make, and
so it coloured the manner of my thought and in that way affected
my actions. On a wet, bleak night in 1972 we went into a bar that
rotated on the top of a high-rise near where I was working. The
maitre d' was clearly unimpressed by us—we were soaking wet

and carelessly dressed—and he gave us a table well separated from the rest of his patrons. It was a good enough harbour, though, and through many slow whiskeys we wrestled in orderly debate. I had proposed that the study of Buddhism be put aside for the dialectics of class struggle. I assumed the role of protagonist first, and he questioned me until my position was clear; then he took the protagonist's role and I questioned him until his position was clear. In this way, in his manner, we debated through the evening, turn and turn again until we had exhaustively compared our worlds. We left the bar at closing time, and the maitre d', who had become interested in us as we talked, wished us a very friendly good night.

The Sanyo building lay in pieces in the clearing for many years. There were problems with paying for it to be assembled. There were problems with deans, boards of directors, faculty heads. There was the problem of who gets the credit. Iida had not made prior arrangements with the university administration. We spoke less and less of the building, although occasionally he would mention that someone had contributed money or that another deadline had been set. Whenever I had business on the campus, I avoided passing by the clearing.

For some months while we were students, my girlfriend and I got into the arrangement of driving him to campus in the mornings. He carried with him a cloth bag containing a length of rope. Each morning at about eight o'clock he would leave us in the parking lot and hike over to the top of the cliffs at the edge of the campus. There he tied the rope to a tree and lowered himself down to the beach. Half an hour later he came back up the rope. While he was down there—he told me this later; I never went with him— he would take off his clothes and wade into the sea. When the water was waist-deep he would lower himself until only his head was above the surface. And then, looking out, he would chant.

Iida's big book was entitled *Reason and Emptiness: A Study in Mysticism and Logic*. My company was preparing the type for his Japanese publisher. It was a difficult job—two-thirds of the text was in Tibetan and Sanskrit—and very slow going. The work was about half done when he appeared in the office one day and demanded a full statement of his account, against which he had been making payments on a casual basis, leaving a growing balance that we had agreed would be payable at some future time. Our bookkeeping methods at that time were rudimentary, and I asked for a couple of days to bring the account up to date. He became agitated and demanded that I do it immediately. I assumed then that he suspected us of some chicanery, and I too became flustered, wondering who could have put this idea in his head. It took my brother and me an hour or more to get the dockets and ledgers collated and to come up with a balance of several hundred dollars. He pulled a roll of bills from his pocket and spilled it on the desk. It was about a hundred short. He asked me to check again, and I offered to call it square with the money on the desk. By now we were both perspiring and the other people in the office were wondering what was going on. Iida refused my offer and so, convinced that some terrible thing had come between us, I started in again on the adding machine. Then the phone rang and it was his wife. He took the receiver and spoke in rapid-fire Japanese. When he hung up, he was visibly changed. He mopped his forehead with his blue handkerchief and leaned back. We can forget this, he said. Everything is all right. I didn't know what to say. He was smiling now. He pushed some of the money across the desk and said to put it on his account in the normal manner. The remainder he pocketed. It would be good to drink a cold beer, he said, and I agreed. We closed down the office and everyone went to the bar. On the way he bought a newspaper, opened it to the second front page, and showed me an article reporting the final installment for the erection of the Asian Studies Centre to have been pledged that morning, by some group in the Japanese community. I paid no attention; I was shaking with relief.

The ritual act of seppuku involves two men dressed in white: first the man sitting cross-legged disembowels himself with a long knife. As he leans forward, having slit his own belly, his "second," who is standing beside him, brings down the long sword and beheads him. It is not uncommon for the second to then impale himself on the sword. The blood is said to be especially vivid against the white cloth.

At the bar, Iida bought all the beer. He was ebullient and said he had one phone call to make. I felt giddy and confused. We were all uneasy and made rather loud small talk, until Iida came back from the phone and brought the conversation around to Mishima's suicide and his old defence of the seppuku ritual. This time he went into the details of preparation: making arrangements for one's family, the composition of a poem to be written in brush strokes on a sheet of rice paper, and the settlement of outstanding debts. When he said this I looked over at my brother and he was looking at me. I felt as if I were turning pale. Surely these things only happen in books. Is that why you came to the office, I said, to settle the account? Iida said: Yes, yes, of course. He pointed to the date on the newspaper. You see the day, he said. Five years today, I made a vow. To raise the money for the building, by today. My brother said, did you write the poem, and Iida said, I have it in my head. Everyone became quiet. Someone said, and the second? I have just called him, said Iida. Everything is off, we can relax now. Later I said to him: now *I* will make a vow to *you*—always to keep your account out of balance. He laughed and said: Yes, yes, of course, you have saved my life.

Five years later, a few weeks before the dedication of the gong in the Asian Studies Centre, Iida appeared in the office and said he had an impossible task for us. The prime minister of Japan, who wrote haiku in his spare time, was coming to make the dedication: could we produce a book of his haiku for the occasion? We had less than three weeks to do it; the book would be in three languages, involving a French translator, an English translator and a dozen calligraphers here and in Japan. Iida said: take the job only if you know you can do it. I said: what is at stake here? And he said:

everything, of course. That night we talked about Iida as much as we talked about the project; our decision to take the project was a decision about Iida. After all, as one of us said, we have nothing to do with prime ministers here.

One Friday night years later, I was on my way up Main Street when I heard a woman's voice call my name. Although I had not seen her for a long time, I knew from years of passing messages on the telephone that the voice belonged to Iida-san's wife—Mrs. Iida, as we called her—and when I turned, there she was, standing in a huddle of people at the bus stop, and Iida was standing beside her. They were on their way to hear a lecture at the city college and were waiting to transfer to the Main Street bus. You've come a long way, I said (their house was about four miles west of where we were standing). It's a good thing you're here, said Mrs. Iida, in a matter-of-fact way (Mrs. Iida is Nisei, and speaks English with no accent that I can hear)—we want you to meet someone important. An elderly couple sitting on the bench were watching us. Iida-san spoke to them in Japanese and they stood up and smiled and bowed toward me. I bowed to them and then we shook hands. The old man was a professor, said Mrs. Iida; we are telling them that you were Iida's first student—you see, Iida was his first student, too. I smiled down at this grey-haired man and this grey-haired woman to whom I could say nothing directly, and bowed again. I felt unusually tall and clumsy and regretful of my ratty torn shirt. As we stood there waiting for the bus, I prayed that it wouldn't be full, but of course it was, and the four of them—Iida-san, his professor and their wives—filed on last to take up positions in the aisle near the driver. As the bus pulled out I continued on my errand, aware—almost painfully so—that, from a certain perspective at least, nothing unusual had happened.

UP CANYON

I took the car and went up the canyon. A simple enough thing to do, when you say it like that: "I think I'll take the car and go up the canyon." I had been meaning to go up the canyon for at least twenty-five years, so a certain pressure had built up when I finally set out one morning late in May. The gas tank was full and there was a box of litre-bottles of 10w30 Eco-oil in the back of the Toyota. I was nervous about the freeway so I stopped at a PetroCan for air and water and gave the kid two bucks to clean the windshield. Then I drove around for a while looking for a bank machine; I was stalling but I knew I was stalling. On the shelf in front of the bank machine someone had left a blank change-of-address card with a Post-It note stuck on it. The message on the Post-It, written in purple ballpoint, said: "Henry, use this to change your address so I won't have to talk to you any more."

By noon I was out at the Trans-Canada, edging into the vehicular stream. The Toyota leapt pleasantly into fourth and slipped into the right-hand lane just before the on-ramp ended. I kept the pedal on the floor as the speedometer crept past the eighty mark. At ninety the front end began to vibrate in a disconcerting way so I eased up and settled my hands on the wheel at ten-to-two and let the needle hover on eighty-five, which I multiplied in my head by six to make it about fifty miles an hour, just enough to maintain one's dignity in the slow lane.

The vehicular stream began to thicken into a kind of high-speed traffic jam as I approached the suburbs and I had to open the window to blow the sweat off my forehead. Cars and trucks tore past in the outside lane and a succession of four-by-fours and ultra-cars loomed up in the rearview before shooting out and around. The noise was terrific; I turned up the FM and hung on as alien street numbers in the high hundreds shot past overhead. Now I was hurtling through the dense exurban perimeter, past wrecking yards and desolate shopping malls bristling with fast food signs, the vacant palisades of industrial parks, and here and there inscrutable patches of leftover greenery. In the distance an enormous pole protruded into the sky, from which a maple leaf flag the size of a tennis court laboured mightily in the breeze. Another overpass rose up ahead: 200th Street, said the green sign in 10,000-point type; I slipped through its shadow like a minnow escaping a net and in moments I was alone on the road with the wind and the radio, and the nearest vehicles were hundreds of yards away. This was the edge of urbanity, then, in a good round number: 200th Street. Now the city and its dominions were behind me; soon I was passing Clearbrook, Raspberry Capital of Canada, and then Chilliwack, which made no claim to be the capital of anything, but included the mayor's phone number on the civic welcome sign. I had been driving for about an hour and already I was in another place; this is what happens when you leave a Canadian city: in very little time you find yourself elsewhere.

I was approaching the town of Hope and the mouth of the canyon when I realized that I had no map. Surely in a canyon a map would be unnecessary, I reasoned. I remembered my friend Enright, who used to go up the canyon every week on his way to Merritt, where he worked for the Nicola Valley Indian Association. You take the right at Spences Bridge, he used to say, that's all you have to know. Enright's preparations for going up the canyon were less diffident than mine. He would drop by my place in the evening and drink beer until midnight, at which time he'd take a big mug of black coffee out to his Volkswagen and head off into the night. At Hope he'd get more coffee at the all-night Mohawk, and then halfway up the canyon he'd take the right turn at Spences Bridge. This was fifteen or sixteen years ago; I had always meant to visit Enright in Merritt in his room at the Coldwater Hotel, but never did.

In Hope I found a coffee shop with an espresso sign, and a woman about my age in a pink apron watched closely as I put sugar and cream into a double espresso and poured it into a plastic cup filled with ice. I've never seen anyone do that before, she said. Neither had I, I realized at that moment. There are only five or six streets in Hope; within a few minutes I had seen them all and no sign of the canyon. Finally I rolled into a service station and confessed to an older guy in a fedora that I was lost. He pushed back the peak of his hat and had me straightened out in no time with a few simple gestures. You get over onto the bridge, you'll be fine, he said. The bridge had one of those wire-ridged surfaces that filled the car with a loud buzz that set my ears tingling; this had always been a thrill when I was a kid in the back seat of the family car, but hadn't they stopped making that kind of bridge years ago? Soon I was among foothills and then the steep shoulders of mountains with snowy peaks. This was the canyon, the Fraser Canyon, and the mountains were the what?—I couldn't remember.

The highway swept me up and down and up again along a ribbon of pavement cut into the edge of the gorge. Occasionally the gorge levelled out into wide green shoulders bearing scatterings of low buildings identified by gnomic signs: Motel Restaurant Lake of the Woods. Cariboo Trail Mobile Home Park Campground RVs. Most of the buildings were a dreary yellow and brown two-tone. And then a long sweeping curve past an enormous empty parking lot and a Husky station with a peeling wooden sign: Breakfast Served All Day. Off to the side a clutch of house trailers sunk into the ground; they too were yellow and brown. A sprinkling of ten-foot satellite dishes pointed at the sky. On the other side of the canyon the sun was shining, but here everything was in shade. There were no people anywhere. Welcome to Historic Yale, Yale Museum and Historic Church. This was Gold Rush country once; what is it now?

At Yale I could see down into the river, which was a swirling chocolate colour; on the other side a creek foamed white as it spilled from a rocky outcrop. Now there were semi-trailers behind and in front of me. We sailed into a tunnel and the air erupted in thunder. I was hanging on now, driving for the bright half-circle at the other end. This was real canyon driving. Out the far end and into the light. Then Saddlerock Tunnel, Sailor Bar Tunnel. Dark, dark, light. Light, light, dark. At Spuzzum I pulled over at the welcome sign to lose the semi-trailers and came to a stop in front of another sign that said Thanks for Visiting Come Again. Then I set off unaccompanied through a further chain of tunnels: Alexandra, Hells Gate, Farrabee, China Bar. Popping out of each of them into a world that seemed each time to be slightly altered, offering a renewed set of hopes and fears. At Boston Bar I stopped for gas next to Roedie's Diner, where there was no espresso machine but a bottomless cup of diner coffee could be had for a dollar. I took mine outside and sipped it at the side of the highway as an erratic stream of semis and pickups and RVs trundled by. So far I hadn't seen anything new in the canyon—nothing newly made, that is. Everywhere the buildings were old and low and wooden, the pavement on the side roads was cracked and worn on the edges, even the satellite dishes were rusty. Only the occasional RV rolling through looked new, and then in an strangely obsolescent way. For nothing of the place itself seemed in any way obsolete; here things were old but familiar, as things were in one's childhood, and I could feel the landscape of my childhood pulling me into itself. On the other side of the river the canyon wall dropped down into a shelf of farmland, or was it ranch land? Someone cultivating something, that's all I could know. Where was the literature of canyon life, canyon culture? What to make of these threadbare stopping places, like the Kanyon View and then the Canyon Alpine, featuring a wall mural of a once-lurid St. Bernard dog wearing lederhosen? Resorts of last resort, perhaps—film noir hideouts for desperadoes on the lam or sad lovers on the run. An RV from New Jersey swept by, Millennium Vacation emblazoned ominously across its back end. I let it get well out of sight before starting up again.

I seemed now to be deep in the canyon, but within a short time the steep bluffs began to recede and the edges of the mountains to soften. By the time I hit Big Horn another, dustier geography was emerging. Big Horn consisted of a single ramshackle building shaped like an oversized igloo with several entrances and a set of Ultra Fuel gas pumps. Discarded tires lay scattered in heaps to one side, and old sofas and stuffed armchairs and broken bicycles lay abandoned in the sagebrush near the igloo-like building. A tall, rather tattered Fruit Stand sign overshadowed the place, and smaller signs listed Ice, Pop, Honey, Fireworks and Canadian Souvenirs in fading red and yellow paint. Inside, a young woman in white poured me a large styrofoam cup of coffee. On the wall behind her hung a notice board covered with foreign inscriptions in black felt pen. That's how to say Thank You in over thirty-five languages, said the young woman. We've had all those languages in here over the years. Thirty-five languages, I said. That last one there is Finnish, she said. That was only last summer. I stared hard at the Finnish inscription as if it might yield up its significance, and the young woman went on to say that her grandmother had the original idea when she had been the Big Horn waitress. That would make three generations, I said, and she nodded and smiled. She seemed strangely older than me. I went outside and took another look around. There was no one else to be seen anywhere in Big Horn. The coffee was bitter and thin and I could hardly swallow it. I drove slowly along the edge of the highway until I was out of sight. Then I opened the door and poured the coffee onto the ground.

At Spences Bridge there didn't seem to be any exact spot where the town started and the country ended. I overshot the intersection and had to back up along the shoulder in order to pick up the right turn to Merritt, as Enright had instructed me so long ago. The turnoff ended a couple of hundred yards from the highway at a long wooden bridge with only one lane. I stopped and peered over the wheel. Surely this wasn't right. I hadn't seen a bridge like this since I was a very small kid. I backed away and drove for a while along the edge of the river looking for the real bridge, which I imagined would be made of steel and maybe have the wire ridges in it. It would definitely have two lanes. But there was no other bridge and soon I was back at the first one, which I knew now to be the only bridge in Spences Bridge. I stopped and looked out over its length. On the other side a ribbon of pavement twisted into the distance, through low hills covered in sagebrush. Then a dusty yellow school bus appeared at the far end of the bridge and began the crossing toward me. I rolled back a few feet, and as the bus neared me it loomed up and then swung to the side and past me, and then it was my turn to use the bridge. I crept out onto the narrow plank surface and accelerated gently. Soon I was in the middle of the bridge, listening to the thrump-thrump-thrump of the wheels on the planks. There was no turning around, but I was excited now: for now I was driving directly into the past.

PILE OF BONES

ENCYCLOPEDIA OF THE
NEW WORLD

The publisher who conceived the idea of the Encyclopedia of the New World suffered from retinitis pigmentosa, a degenerative condition of the retinal nerve, and when I met him in 1980 he had lost ninety percent of his vision and had to carry a white cane when he went to strange cities. I first laid eyes on him when he walked past the window of the office in which we had arranged to meet and then five minutes later walked by again in the other direction, this time carrying the white cane, and I went out onto the sidewalk and introduced myself. He was a son of the Nuu-chah-nulth nation, and his grandparents at a fourth or fifth remove had not been among the first discoverers of Captain Cook, as they lived in a village farther along the coast; it was people from a neighbouring village who found Captain Cook floating on the ocean in a boat as big as a house, with not a drop of water left to drink, in March of 1778. Captain Cook named the place in which he was found, and in which his thirst was quenched, by taking a phrase from the local language which he understood to be the name of the place, but which when translated meant "you are going around in circles"; this was *Nootka*, the name inscribed by Captain Cook on the map of a world from which the fabulous Sea of Anian and the North-west Passage would finally be erased. The Nuu-chah-nulth people, perceiving their visitors to have no dry land of their own, referred to Captain Cook and his crew with a word that translates as *floaters*, a term for Europeans that is still in use today. The Encyclopedia of the New World would be the story of the people whose world had been remade by strangers from Europe quick to name their own world *old* as soon as they encountered another one.

The publisher and I became friends and I went with him to Toronto where he wished to receive the advice of other publishers who were meeting in a darkly panelled, dimly lit room in an expensive downtown hotel. It was precisely the dark panelling and the intimate lighting, which had been designed to put us at ease, that put my friend at a disadvantage, for he was unable in such darkness to see anything at all, and as I watched him making his way uneasily through the murky passageways of the expensive hotel, I felt the sighted world withdrawing itself from him and his great purpose. It was winter and we went on to Ottawa on the train through the bright Canadian snowscape that we both recognized from photographs in the textbooks of our school days. In Ottawa my friend interviewed smiling bureaucrats who had many things on their minds, and then we had our photograph taken as we waved our hands in front of the houses of Parliament, in colourful toques that we had brought with us especially for the occasion.

Some years went by and my friend began a new publishing operation on Vancouver Island and spoke less frequently of the Encyclopedia which had come to occupy much of his thinking. I heard nothing from him for a few years; then last month I saw his name on the front page of the newspaper, which identified him as "spokesman for the natives" who had succeeded in a civil suit against the government and the United Church for crimes committed against them when they were children in a residential school. The school had been at Port Alberni (which is named for the officer who led the Spanish occupation of Nootka in 1791), and the children who once resided there were taken from homes up to a thousand miles away. I called up my friend and he told me that his sight was completely gone now and that he and his wife and friends had been organizing for the trial for a long time, arranging healing feasts at which people who had never spoken aloud about what had happened to them as children were able for the first time to tell their stories. The largest of these gatherings numbered seven hundred people, before whom his wife, whose name is Edith, cut off her long hair, which I remembered to be beautiful and dark and very long, and made it a gift to the great healing that was underway. I understood as he was telling me this that the Encyclopedia of the New World had never been abandoned; instead it had taken on a new and more urgent form.

My friend's name is Randolph, and he once told me that he had been named by his parents after a Hollywood actor of the strong silent type much admired in Western movies. This would have been just after the period in which the comic strip character for whom my parents named me—an American fighter pilot whose last name was Canyon—had become even more popular than the Katzenjammer Kids.

PATINA

I walked through downtown Regina and within an hour or so the place began to seem familiar in its outward aspect: a railroad station in the middle of town, a glimpse of park, a scattering of pawn shops nearby, a dun-coloured parking building. A glockenspiel thrashing tunes into the cold air of a Friday night. All was brown and the automobiles were universally coated with mud and dust. I could hear in voices on the sidewalk the occasional lilt of another way of speaking, with flattened vowels, and a rhythm made of longer beats, but soon I heard it no more. So easily do we become accustomed to the nearly familiar. Within a day I was settled in, comfortable with the pattern of the downtown streets—the route from the hotel to my few destinations: who that lived here knew the place as superficially as I did? The question made me self-conscious and I was aware of not seeing what was surely there to be seen.

A few days later, in Saskatoon, I sat at the round table by the window on the third floor of the Park Town Motor Lodge and looking out at a stretch of river still partially covered in ice. A bit of yellow-brown grass (what was that colour?—I had no name for it), a few leafless trees, a pale sand-coloured bridge. The sky was white, shading to a pale blue in the north. In the foreground cars and trucks covered with dust to the gunnels swept around a loop of grey pavement. I went outside and looked again at the pavement and saw that it was not really grey; it was brown, and so was the sidewalk. I hiked up a grassy knoll to the statue of Gabriel Dumont and when I got there my shoes, which had been clean when I set out, were covered in brown dust. I stooped to look at them and wanted to brush them off and then I saw that each blade of grass at my feet carried a fine coating of the same brown dust; I combed through the grass with my fingers and a film of grit came away on my hand. This was what I had not yet seen in these two prairie cities: the dust which lay on every surface. I stood up and looked out over the dusty surface of Saskatoon, and at the dusty surface of the statue of Gabriel Dumont standing next to me. What this untidy place needed, I couldn't help thinking, was a spring cleaning, a good dusting off with a giant feather duster.

Now dust was everywhere in my vision and I wondered how it was perceived by those who lived with it. Was there a kind of beauty in the dust that an outsider was unable to perceive? I began asking questions of the publishers and the editors with whom I was working, but none of them were willing to admit that the dust, which they agreed was everywhere to be seen, had any aesthetic significance. One of them suggested that perhaps the dust could be seen as a harbinger of spring, but this reply was given more to soothe than to enlighten me. The plainest response (and one that seemed to render my question harmless) was given by an editor of literary fiction who said: dust is what we live with in Saskatchewan.

Then at dinner in an Italian restaurant the publisher of *The Wheatgrass Mechanism* told me that the dust I had been concerning myself with was not native prairie dust at all; it was merely the residue of the sand and gravel dumped on the roads during the winter. His reply was an evasion of my question, but nevertheless I wondered why no one else had told me this. He then described with some heat what he said was true prairie dust, a fine black material that occurs early in the summer, when the wind picks up the topsoil and the air becomes dark with it. The effect of this dust, which gets into your teeth and ears and seeps in through every crack in the wall and covers everything in the house, he said, is to drive you crazy. He became rather passionate on the subject, and as his voice rose I could hear diphthongs forming within his plain Canadian vowels. After a short interval I asked if he was perhaps from Nova Scotia and he said that he was; he had been living in Saskatchewan for the last three years. We were the only customers in the restaurant and when our meal was ended we asked our waitress, a girl of about twelve, for coffee and brandy. She brought the coffee and then disappeared behind the bar; some minutes passed and then she called out to say that she had run out of brandy. This seemed unlikely, as we had observed her take down a nearly full bottle of Hennesey's from the shelf. We went over and looked down at the table behind the bar where she had set out two large beer glasses, one of which was filled to the brim and the other about half way. The brandy bottle, which she held out to us, was empty. The publisher of *The Wheatgrass Mechanism* looked at her and said, she's quite right, of course: she has run out of brandy.

When I got home to Vancouver it had been raining earlier in the day and now the weather was clearing as I peered through the window of the taxi at gleaming black streets and green boulevards. The sun broke through the clouds and for a moment in the radiant light I detected a harshness in the look of things here that I had never seen before: the grass was suddenly too green, the sky, where it was clearing, too blue, and the wet pavements were unacceptably lustrous; all was overstated and I could see an unpleasant boldness in this place where I live. As soon as I looked again, it was all gone, and things had become, as too frequently they do, merely familiar.

ICE STORM

We left Halifax on Saturday morning, in a rented car in the rain, bound for Fredericton and the alien province of New Brunswick. We had a couple of days of contract work in Fredericton and wanted time to hang around there before the work started. Heavy cloud lay close above us and the rain was hard and thin but nothing to worry about; Mary had the wheel and I had the map and a bag of dulse lay open on the back seat. We weren't too sure about the dulse: the label said nothing about what the stuff was, although it identified the bag, a kind of crinkly cellophane, as "photo-degradable and bio-degradable." The clerk at the hotel had said to us, "Well, it's *dulse*, you know," and we had nibbled on a bit of it while watching the late news. The dulse was salty and stuck to our teeth but then it softened up and went down all right with a couple of bottles of Moosehead Beer.

The car was one of those generic compacts with a low roof and a hatchback and nowhere to put your legs, but it got us to Truro in good time. The rain seemed to be thickening as we swept up the one-way ramp onto the Trans-Canada, and the water on the road seemed to be thicker too if that was possible. Mary took her foot off the gas and we slowed into the curve and directly into the path of a tiny yellow car that was drifting around the same curve the wrong way toward us. Before we could stop, the yellow car jerked to the side, slipped slowly over the shoulder and fell nose down into the

ditch. We pulled over and stopped. The rear end of the yellow car
was stuck up over the shoulder and its doors opened and three
young men climbed out of it. Everything seemed terribly peaceful;
all we could hear was the heavy drumming of rain on the roof.
Then another tiny car, a red one, swept past us from behind and
fishtailed into the curve, whacked into the back of the yellow car
and drifted to a stop. Then it was quiet again. I opened the door
and stepped out onto the edge of the road and my feet shot out
from under me; I threw an arm over the top of the door as the
muscles in my groin heaved dangerously. At my feet the gravel
lay unmoving beneath a glistening layer of clear glass that spread
out onto the asphalt and across the road; a moment passed before
I understood that the world was covered in ice. I hung onto the
door of the car and called out to the young men; one of them
waved and said they could manage without us. They were moving
carefully and they seemed to be unconcerned by the ice that was
falling all around them. I got back into the car and my glasses were
covered in ice and there was ice in my hair. Mary got us going and
eased us slowly along the ramp onto the Trans-Canada. The
world outside seemed utterly calm; there was no wind, there was
no whistling or buffetting: just the steady falling of white icy rain
from the sky.

We pressed on for another hour at low speed and an endless
procession of eighteen-wheelers thundered past us in the outside
lane, throwing up great sheets of liquid ice that fell over us with a
crash, and I remembered something from school about ice getting
thick when you might expect it to get thin. Gradually ice began to
collect on the road, and soon we could hear brashy slush scraping
the bottom of the car. When we crossed into New Brunswick the
ice was piling up on the windshield and the wipers were heaving
wearily, clearing off a diminishing series of half moons through
which we peered into a relentless scrub forest of tangled treelike
materials; here the Trans-Canada began its endless climb west-
ward; there was no sign of organized life anywhere save for the

occasional abandoned car that lay in the ditch beside the road, and the stream of vehicles overtaking us from behind. Mary maintained a steady jogging speed and we burrowed along with our heads pressed forward to our spyholes in the windshield, wincing each time another car sped past, fishtailing wildly into the distance. At one point I glanced back to see an overtaking car shoot across the road and into the ditch. A few moments later Mary looked up at the rearview and said, "There goes another one." All around us seemed to be developing an increasing level of hazard, something neither of us could understand to be a storm, and with it some species of psychotic event unfolding in the collective mind of New Brunswickers bent on throwing themselves into the teeth of it.

After a very long time the impervious black wall of scrimpy forest yielded space enough for a truck stop, and we pulled in to the cafe for sandwiches and coffee and a chance to suppress our panic without appearing to have to do so. In the cafe we scrutinized the road map: if there was any point of no return on this wretched stretch of the Trans-Canada, we were now at it. The cafe was filled with calm people, none of whom appeared to have anything to say to their tablemates; the only sound in the place was the murmur of the waitresses and the radio bleating soft rock from a shelf behind the counter. When the music stopped a chirpy voice proclaimed a "storm weather warning" to be "in effect throughout the area." Mary and I lowered our voices to whisper level. I wanted to know if these people lived nearby, at least the waitresses, the gas jockeys over at the pumps. Sandwiches appeared before us: if we ran to the car now we might get a jump on whatever lay ahead; but at the same time we needed this break. Mary's eyes were completely round. Whatever we do, she said, I know how to drive in this now. I felt relieved but horribly compromised: Mary was lying and I had to accept the lie she was offering; I was too frightened to drive, and unwilling to talk about it. We finished the sandwiches and the chirpy radio voice broke in on our deliberations: "All weather warnings are now cancelled," the voice said. "All previous warnings are no longer in effect." All right, we whispered. Let's get to Moncton and call it a day.

The thick white stuff was still falling out of the sky and there were icicles hanging from the smooth round surface of the rented car which we would have thought could have no edges; enormous icicles hung from the truck-stop sign next to the road and sheets of ice were draped from the transmission wires. Everything was deathly quiet. I smashed the ice away from the headlights and Mary rolled us over to the gas pumps, where an older guy with ice in his hair stooped down to look in at us.

MARY: Would you take a swipe at those wipers, please?

OLDER GUY: Sure enough, you got to shake them up, break the ice off like this. Real careful. Got a few in today snapped them right off. They freeze up and break, you know, storm like this one. We don't sell wipers here, so you need wipers now, you'd be out of luck.

MARY: How much longer you think this'll go on?

OLDER GUY: Well how far you going? Moncton?

MARY: Moncton.

OLDER GUY: Oh well all the way easy, all the way to Moncton at least. It'll be bad getting to Moncton. You can count on it.

MARY: Okay. All the way to Moncton then.

OLDER GUY: You got her.

The ice on the road had built up enough to fasten onto the drive train from time to time and throw the car from one side of the lane to the other but there were fewer speeders now, and only the occasional roaring semi-trailer. It was getting dark and the falling ice was getting thicker, and soon we could see only a few yards down the road. Whenever it seemed safe to stop, I'd get out and shake the wipers up and down the way the guy at the truck stop had done it. Then I'd clear the ice from the headlights and taillights. This was the least I could do but it was also all I could do, and I began to feel a growing resentment toward the national highway. When we got to Moncton it was pitch dark and the ice was still falling out of the sky, but there were lights along the streets and we could see where the frozen snow lay in heaps too big to navigate. Mary poked a course into the centre of the city and nudged us into a frozen snowdrift outside the Hotel Colonial something. I leapt out and my socks filled up with ice as I made my way through to the sidewalk. Inside the Colonial at the reception desk there were two women who seemed astonished to see me.

ME: Have you a room, please?

OLDER WOMAN: No.

(Long pause.)

OLDER WOMAN: There are no rooms.

ME: You're booked up?

OLDER WOMAN: There are no rooms in Moncton.

ME: Perhaps you can direct me to another hotel.

OLDER WOMAN: There *are no rooms* in Moncton. (Her gaze is steely. She looks directly into my eyes.)

YOUNGER WOMAN (also looking directly into my eyes): Umhmm. (Both women—gloating?—continue to gaze into my eyes.)

I went out into the snow and got back in the car. Mary circled a couple of blocks and stopped at another hotel. Inside a lone woman stood at the counter. She was all dressed up and seemed to be waiting for her date, and I remembered that it was Saturday night.

She too seemed surprised to see me.

WOMAN: Oh, we don't have any rooms!

ME: How can there be no rooms in a big city like this?

WOMAN: Oh, it's the carpenters, they've got all the rooms!

ME: (Silence.)

WOMAN: Oh.

ME: So there really are no rooms in Moncton.

The city of Moncton had turned against us. There was ice in my hair and my ears were freezing. Mary nosed the car along the grim streets as I manipulated the road map in the light from the dash; slowly we made our way toward the Trans-Canada, along bleak avenues of car lots and motels with bright No Vacancy signs. Our hearts were turned against this place forever. A last motel rose up in the murk, the No Vacancy shimmering beneath a name: Beacon Light Motel. Let's pull in here, I said, we'll talk to them anyway. Mary nudged the car into a snowdrift and turned off the ignition. She was looking straight ahead.

The air in the office of the Beacon Light smelled like roast beef and potatoes. Behind the counter an older woman was talking on the phone. She watched me come in and then hung up and said right out, "Oh dear, you could use a cup of coffee." I went out to the car to snap Mary out of her trance. In the Beacon Light a silent teenaged girl handed us two big mugs of instant coffee. The woman was saying, "Oh dear, well what can we do?" Then she got back on the phone and started calling motels up the road until she got one with a vacancy eleven miles out. We sipped our coffee and she talked about the storm. "Five people dead on the Trans-Canada so far," she said. "This is a real bad one." The carpenter convention was the first ever in Moncton; that's why the carpenters got all the rooms. The teenaged girl lounged against the wall, examining us silently. We went back to the car and the air was thick with ice. Mary asked me if I had noticed the shirts that the kind woman and her daughter were wearing. They were covered in handwriting, she said. All in ballpoint. I hadn't noticed a thing.

Now we were at the far end of Moncton, where there were no signs to direct us out of town, but we had our direction from the Beacon Light and so made our way back onto the Trans-Canada with our hearts softened toward the bitter city of Moncton. We pressed on at twenty miles an hour, wipers straining mightily against the falling ice. Before us lay two ruts in the highway: all else was ice and snow. Mary let the ruts carry us forward; we could see only a few yards into the night. Eventually a blur of neon loomed in the distance and then we could make out the words: Drink Coca Cola Motel. As we drew near we could see the icicles covering the Vacancy sign. Mary threw the wheel over and gunned it and we shot over the sludge and into a driveway; a few minutes later we were ensconced in Unit Nine, a cinderblock room with red indoor- outdoor on the floor and bits of glitter in the ceiling, a true haven in a storm.

The next morning the sky was clear and blue and the land was blindingly white—a quintessentially Canadian day. The whole enormous parking lot of the Drink Coca Cola Motel had been scraped bare of snow and ice, as had the Trans-Canada itself, as we discovered after fastening our seat belts and our clip-on sunglasses and pulling out into the dry pavement of the national highway. Later we stopped to talk to a man driving a miniature bulldozer. He was wearing tiny round sunglasses and seemed to have been waiting for us to show up. "That was some storm we had last night," he said. "You coming up from Halifax? You'll hear the French language spoken here, you know. Now you take my daughter, she's a university graduate, eh? But she never got the bilingual so she had to go down the road. That's the story here. Got herself a job in Toronto, twenty-nine thousand a year just like that. You gotta go down the road, I been here all my life. That's the whole story, you know." Later we remembered the dulse, which was still in the back seat, and for some reason that made me think of Magnetic Hill and the Tidal Bore, things of Moncton that now we would never see.

PILE OF BONES

It was forty below in Regina in December, and I could feel my kneecaps freezing at the bus stop in front of Eaton's, where I had been waiting a long time for the RCMP bus, and I wondered if I should go inside and buy some long underwear. When the bus arrived it filled up with shoppers with red cheeks and rustling packages, and I found a seat at the back opposite three young men wearing shiny black shoes who were conversing quietly in French. Within minutes we were at the edge of the downtown core, and the cold air beyond the window seemed to be stealing the colour away first from storefronts, and now low pale housefronts surrounded by a dusting of dirty snow and the sparse blue shadows of leafless trees. People began getting off at deserted intersections as the bus crept through a network of silent suburban streets, and when we crossed the freeway at the edge of the city, only the young men speaking French were left on board with me. For a few minutes we could see the modest towers of the city under a pallid sky and then the bus turned away into an expanse of white fields through which the road before us rose up in a straight, vertiginous line to a flat horizon. In the middle distance lay a scattering of low buildings; here the bus pulled over and the doors clattered open, and we stepped out in cold twilight onto the grounds of the RCMP barracks, police college and museum.

As I stood at the side of the bus trying to get my bearings, a burst of orchestral music exploded above our heads, and the over-amplified voice of Bing Crosby dreaming of a white Christmas erupted into the silent afternoon. I turned to look at the young men who had been speaking French, but they had moved away, and now they were striding purposefully into the compound toward the source of that ear-splitting clamour, which resembled the sound of a forty-five-gallon drum tumbling down a fire escape. The monstrous noise continued to pour undiminished over the prairie and I realized that the young men had not come to this place, as I had, to rubberneck; they had come to serve. I set off alone in another direction, like a man swimming underwater, pressing on through the torrent of sound until I came to the RCMP Museum, which had been my destination all along; as the two sets of glass doors swung closed behind me, the lenses in my spectacles sheeted over and I felt myself coming up for air into a blurry warm silence of blue carpets and beige walls.

The RCMP Museum had been unknown to me until earlier in the day, when I first noticed the RCMP bus in the streets of Regina, and which I decided to board after learning its destination. Now I had arrived at the house of memory, in the western headquarters of the world's only souvenir police force, and when I put my spectacles back on, an older, heavy-set man in a blue uniform shirt and dark blue trousers appeared before me and said, So you're alone then, as if he had been expecting me to bring a friend. He waved a hand toward an open doorway behind him and told me to go on in anyway; I thanked him and stepped through into a dimly lit corridor that opened into a narrow room lined with glass cabinets.

All was silence in the narrow room; I could hear only my own breathing. The cabinets on the walls contained leather garments, presumably of Native origin, many of them embroidered and decorated with beads and quills, none of them identified. Ahead were cabinets filled with weaponry: pistols and rifles, sabres; and then pieces of uniform: helmets, gloves, boots and tunics; a tray full of medals; a few saddles; a few brass telescopes. I passed silently through this mute display to a turning in the far wall, which brought me to a pile of cannonballs and a cannon, a few mortars, and a wall covered in huge photographs of men with moustaches identified with little name cards: Wentworth, Kittson, Nicole, Clark, Allan, Walker, Welch, Macleod. I wrote them down in my notebook for reasons that I can no longer remember and went on to a button in the wall next to a note that said "Push to hear an RCMP waltz." I pushed the button and the sound of a brass band blasted into the passageway in three-quarter time. I froze where I stood, and I wondered if the man in the blue shirt could hear it through the wall. Abruptly the music stopped and all was silent again.

I was beginning to feel a deadening of the senses and a kind of claustrophobia as I pressed on through more turnings in the walls, past discarded uniforms mounted on wire frames, stuffed animals in bits of papier-maché landscape, more saddles, and then a large grainy photograph of a fort in front of which Native families were sitting in the grass. A note beside the photograph said "Fort Whoop-up, a whisky trading post." I looked for more notes on the wall, but there were none; nothing of what, when or even where Fort Whoop-up was. Farther on a neatly lettered sign appeared on the wall: "Pile of Bones," it said, "1873." Here was a glimmering of narrative, at least a time, a place. The accompanying photograph depicted a blank stretch of prairie empty of human beings next to a floor plan sketch of a small fortress. No doubt the two were connected, but the teller of this story was refusing to make the commitment. A few feet farther along another placard on the wall said "Sitting Bull's New Home, 1877," and nothing of Sitting Bull's old home; in the cabinet beneath it lay a beaded rifle case and a leather bag, objects identified in another note that said nothing about what they were doing in the cabinet, as "once belonging to Sitting Bull." I felt again a glimmering of a narrative withheld, and I began to understand that no story would be given here in this place, where the objects of memory were mere dots in a child's puzzle. Here, if you wanted a story, you had to make it up as you went.

Now there were documents framed on the wall: treaties six and seven, according to the note. What of numbers one to five? I wanted to ask. Nothing else was given, save the opportunity to read for myself the full text of treaties six and seven. I passed on to more placards: Batoche, Louis Riel, The Boer War. Now there were paintings on the walls, made by officers behind the front lines, and here was a piece of the noose that broke Riel's neck, and the sword that had belonged to the son of Charles Dickens, who is credited in an unusually long note (perhaps because Dickens seems to have been the closest thing to a celebrity in the Force) with having saved "women and children from Indian atrocities." It was unclear from the display how any of these things were connected. The Boer War was illustrated by a photograph of men who were presumably Mounties, with no explanation of what Canadian policemen were doing in South Africa in a war. Through turning after turning the placards went on: The Great War, Vladivostok, The Communist Party, 1935: Regina, World War II, The Musical Ride: nowhere in this procession were the structures of cause and effect expressed or implied.

As I made my way farther into the maze, I had the unsettling impression that I was being led deep underground and that the ceiling was getting closer to my head: the Klondike; the Lost Patrol; the Gatling gun, a random litter of handcuffs, ball and chain, ankle weights, small arms and ammunition. I pushed another button to hear the Dinsmore Gallop "as performed by the Musical Ride": another blast from a brass band, another abrupt return to silence. Here was a glass case filled with ceremonial pipes: whose had they been? I would never know. Here were decks of playing cards and German war paraphernalia, photographs of the trenches in World War I, then a swastika and a placard that said simply, "World War II." (How did the Mounties get into all these wars?) Under the photograph of uniformed men on a pier in Vladivostok, a note of coyness could be detected in the caption, which identified the occasion (in reality, the botched invasion of Russia in 1919) as "an opportunity for the Force to achieve an advanced state of preparedness."

At some point in this dreamlike passage, I remember bending down in an offhand way to peer into a stereoscopic viewer set into a plastic box at a height low enough for children to reach, and as the bright light inside the viewer hit my eyes I felt all the heaviness around me vanish in an instant. Now I was standing on the prairie (so convincing is the three-dimensional rendering of the stereo-scope) and there was a patch of tall grass in front of me and beyond it a cluster of eight Native men sitting on the ground, looking back at me patiently; behind them were tepees and wagons. Two of the men nearest me were bare-chested and I could see that they were composed of flesh and bone because I could feel it in my eyes. This apparition of reality was so powerful that I thrust out a hand and felt myself falling into that space before my hand collided with the plastic box. When I stood up there were tears in my eyes. I had not been prepared for this.

There were two or three such viewers set into boxes nearby and I looked cautiously into them and felt myself transported each time into another place: in particular, a stable in which men in mous-taches were tending horses; I apprehended them in the intimate space of the viewer to be very young men somewhat awkwardly trying to be grown up; they looked vulnerable in their undershirts and partially buttoned tunics, as they raised their arms over the horses to place a blanket, to run a brush over a muscled back; they would never know that I was watching them.

I did not wish to go on, but I felt unable to linger among these hallucinatory scenes. I stood up and pushed another button in the wall and the sound of a locomotive building up steam and blowing its whistle issued from a speaker near the ceiling; a few feet away hung a large placard bearing the following pronouncement: "Riel's

Manitoba Rebellion was doomed to failure, as the CPR was fated to succeed." I had to stop and read it again: surely this was a grand thematic statement, joining in a single sentence the will of God with the actions of providence, and bearing in mind that the fates of men and institutions are foreknown only by inscrutable destiny. Here was the key to the puzzle: the "story" of the Force was to be framed within the struggle of the titans Riel and the CPR, and to be determined by destiny. The birth of the RCMP, then, was merely the consequence for which Riel and the CPR provided the initial conditions. Perhaps this was all we needed to know.

At the next turning my way was blocked by an enormous plastic cylinder set in the middle of the floor; inside the cylinder a dozen or more makeshift cudgels dangled weirdly on lengths of fishing line. The placard above it said "1935 Regina," and a brief hermetic text mentioned the arrest of "two main Communist agitators" otherwise unnamed. After that there were snowshoes, parkas, a stuffed husky dog; an absurd larger-than- life photograph of the commissioner and J. Edgar Hoover, both of them grinning fiercely; a model of the *St. Roch*; a full- scale phone booth (why a phone booth?—I didn't pause); and in the final turning, the pre-served corpse of a fully grown horse standing in a huge plexiglass box: all that remains of the stallion Nero, according to the placard, once beloved of the Force. Off to the side were tear gas guns, tear gas machine guns and a tear gas billy club. I stepped around Nero and into the corridor, and then I was back in the lobby of the museum, and there was the older man in the blue uniform shirt, sitting on a sofa against the wall, waiting for me. He looked sleepy and relaxed, and I was relieved to see him there.

Over the following days and weeks I thought often of the people I had seen in the stereoscopic viewers in the strange museum of the RCMP, and just as often I remembered the older man in the blue shirt. He was a plain-looking man with a belly, and when he got up from the sofa and stepped toward me his face was open and without malice or guile.

WANDERING BOY

An old guy in one of those racing caps that look like berets from a distance got on the train at Winnipeg with his wife, and once he had her settled in he began strolling up and down the aisle looking out the windows in the manner of an art gallery patron looking at paintings on a wall. He was short and stout and wore a poplin windbreaker of the kind that one associates with grandfathers or small businessmen taking their leisure on a Sunday afternoon. The train had been moving for half an hour and the landscape had begun to deteriorate into scrub and rock and pale evergreens and ominous flat pools of water. My berth was at the far end of the car, and as no one had taken the upper I was alone in the double seat when the old guy leaned over my shoulder to take a long look at the scene in my window, and then he said, that's Caddy Lake out there, you know. Pickerel, whitefish, jackfish too, of course. I was surprised to learn that such a place had any name at all and when I asked him what it meant he said he'd always figured someone must have dropped a tea caddy in it, if I knew what he meant by a tea caddy, which is something you don't see much of these days.

Then he told me that jackfish can make good eating, but only in cold water. They're no good at all in warm water, he said with a certain emphasis. If I wanted lake trout, I'd have to go farther north. The lakes we were looking at were too shallow: you needed a deep lake for trout and for that I'd have to go north, where I could take a lake trout twenty, thirty pounds on a good day. Then he began to instruct me in the art of fly fishing, for which he supplied me with many details too esoteric to be remembered when I was alone later with my notebook. He spoke in a forthright way, leaning over and looking out my window and then over to the next window and back to mine. Now he had his hands on the backs of my seat and the next one over, and I felt obscurely protected as he hovered over me while the train wound through a sodden and alien landscape.

When the train stopped at Kenora, he dropped into the seat facing me to get a closer look into a town that he said he had known well when he used to travel from Port Arthur to Winnipeg, before Port Arthur became Thunder Bay. In Kenora, he said, they had a hell of a time with the Indians, who used to get a load on and then tear hell out of the place. Now they don't let them in the beer parlours, he said, so they drink over in the back there now. He waved a hand toward what I took to be the back of Kenora, and I looked over that way for a while as he talked about coming out to Kenora in the dirty thirties when they used to ride the boxcars. One summer he and some buddies decided to take a holiday. One of them had an old canoe which they carried down to the CPR yards, and they were getting it strapped onto a boxcar when a cop spotted them and came running over.

What do you boys think you're doing with that canoe? said the cop.

Why we're going on a holiday, officer. Can't you tell?

It was the damndest thing that cop ever saw.

The old guy lived with his wife on Lake Winnipeg in a cottage that he insulated himself with vapour barriers, styrofoam and fibreglass, and they could live there all year long if they had to. But they liked to travel, and so in the summers they travelled on the wife's pension and in the winter they travelled on his. In this way they had gone to Australia and New Zealand and then twelve times to Florida. Now they were on their way to Spain and the Canary Islands, which they had never seen. He had wanted to go to Spain ever since 1936, which was the year his granny died in Winnipeg and he got home too late for the funeral. That night he went down to the beer parlour and met some buddies who were drinking with a recruiter for the Spanish Civil War, and before closing time they had all agreed to meet the recruiter at the CN station in the morning and set off to join the fight against Franco. One of the great regrets in his life was that he never made it down to the station that morning in 1936, he said, but he and his best buddy had thought it was just the beer talking, so they let it go. Some of the other guys went ahead with it, though, and in three months all of them were dead.

He had been making steel out west, fifteen hundred miles from home, and he was climbing the ladder up to the crusher, where you have these little baskets and you put the coal in them and they go up to the high line and then over and down. He was halfway up to the highliner first thing in the morning, when he turned to the man behind him and said, Pal, I'm going home right now. It's my granny. He climbed down and cashed in and hit a freight train home. He got into Winnipeg five hours after the funeral.

She was really his father's aunt, not his grandmother at all, but everyone had always called her Little Granny. Before she died she was heard to say, "Where is my wandering boy?" and everyone knew who she meant, for he was the black sheep of the family and no one knew where the hell he was when he was up on the highliner fifteen hundred miles away and he had what he said was a kind of vision of Little Granny. They figured out the timing and it seemed to add up.

His father had been what they called a real clean liver. No smoke, no drink, no cards. He was a Scot and his parents had been among the founders of Guelph, Ontario. His father read the Bible aloud before dinner and after dinner, like it or not, and he went to church Sunday morning, Sunday night, Wednesday night, and

Friday night too, and the strongest curse he ever used was: scissors and groundhogs, confound it! He was out putting up fence, and the hired man was standing in the wagon so he could hit the post hard from above, and the old man was holding the post. He put his hand up on the top of the post when he thought it was in far enough, and the hired man brought the hammer down one more time and broke all the bones in his hand. Well, the old man just stomped around in a circle, moving his hand up and down real slow, growling scissors and groundhogs, confound it, scissors and groundhogs, over and over again. That hired man used to laugh when he told that story.

Later that afternoon the scene beyond my window had devolved into a fierce stubble of short, tattered evergreens extending out over a quagmire of mud and water toward low hills in the distance. Then a series of shattered power poles began stepping past the window and there were power lines lying in the water and then an entire freight train lying on its side in an enormous trench half filled with water. It looked as if it had been thrown off the embankment and abandoned where it lay. In an instant it was gone. I was making notes about the old guy, who had gone back to check on his wife, and I didn't think about that train again until reading my notes a week later.

The old guy appeared again in the aisle and said that he wanted me to know that eventually he did go to war, the big one, double-you double-you two. He signed up in 1941 and didn't come home until Christmas Day, 1944, at ten o'clock in the morning. He loved that war and he wanted to go back a week later, but they weren't sending anyone back by that time. He had been an air mechanic, coastal, moving around all the time from drome to drome.

They used to put bombs under those dromes, he said, with three or four controls for each one, in case Heinie took over. The WAFS didn't like that. They were getting pregnant just to get the hell out of there. For the first couple of years they sent the WAFS home if they got up a stump, and that was it, which was fine with a lot of them, apparently. There was a guy with red hair and a big red beard, the women loved him. He got twenty-nine of them pregnant in two months. He was a stingy guy, very cheap. Cheap guys make it with women for some reason, the old guy didn't know why. Then they were down in Cornwall and there was a Heinie coming over every day at eleven o'clock in the morning. He'd make a big circle and swoop down over the town, and empty a bag of nuts and bolts over the side. It was some kind of a joke. You could see him holding the bag out over the side. Just nuts and bolts. When they finally shot him down the whole town got upset because they'd taken such a liking to the guy.

When he was young he had worked on a tugboat on the west coast, up the inside passage with a crew of eight, five of whom were named Olson, and they called each other Ole. It was his job to round them up when they got drunk on shore. At one time there had been a famous moose near Kenora, known as the Lily Pond moose, and back in about 1929 an even more famous moose that used to come down to meet the train outside of Jasper, Alberta. This moose became known all over the world and trains would slow down so people could take pictures of it. Then one day it went mad and charged the train, and the Mounties took the dogs into the bush and tracked it down and shot it. He had heard of another moose that delivered the mail somewhere in the Yukon, but he couldn't remember exactly when that had been.

When it got dark outside, the old guy went back to his wife to arrange for dinner. Later that night in the bar car, he said that I could call him Pop, because everyone called him that and I probably wouldn't remember his name anyway. He had been meaning to tell me about the Castle in the Woods, which we had passed a few hours ago and which had been built by a man with a broken heart, and also about a lost prehistoric world that lay beneath the Columbia Icefield. We drank a couple of beers and a young man I had been talking to, who said he was a lawyer on his way to Toronto to look for legal business, picked up his glass and went to sit at another table. I asked Pop to write his address for me on a matchbook so that I could send him this story if I ever wrote it up. He wrote down his initials and an address in Manitoba, and in the morning after he and his wife had changed trains, the matchbook was gone and I never saw it again.

In 1931 when he and his best buddy were in New Brunswick, they went over to the U.S. side and got arrested roasting potatoes in a field. They were put in jail in some hamlet and there was no lock on the door to the cell. One of the other prisoners was a bootlegger whose mother came into the cell and beat him up for getting arrested. She was a logger woman with hair on her chest, six feet tall, two hundred pounds, and the bootlegger was the toughest man in town. There was another guy in there, a little soft in the head, who looked like a monkey. He had helped himself to someone else's dinghy in the harbour when his own dinghy drifted away on him. And a young kid, Pop said he didn't know why the kid was in jail. But this kid, he'd sit on the monkeyman's lap and shave the hair off the guy's face with a straight razor, no lather, just pulling the blade down, real gentle, careful, you know, his arms up like this. It was enough to bring tears to your eyes, watching those two, he said. I'll never forget it.

ONCE IN EATONIA

When my grandfather was twenty-four, in 1912, the Eaton's Athletic Association, for which he played right field, won the Intermediate Baseball Championship in Winnipeg. In the photograph commemorating the event, my grandfather can be seen standing at the left of a line of young men wearing what now appear to be old-fashioned uniforms. I recognize him by his nose, which resembles my brother's. Of course he is not yet my grandfather in the photograph; he is a clerk in the mail order department, and his job is to fill orders that come in from the Eaton's catalogue. A few years after the photograph was taken, my grandfather joined the army to fight in the Great War, and Eaton's paid him a half salary (as they did all single employees who joined up for that war; married men got full salaries) until, having survived the trenches as a private in France, he was able to return to Eaton's and to his job. It is no surprise that my grandfather remained loyal to Eaton's and that he passed his working life there; after twenty-five years he was awarded a gold pocket watch, and when he retired he was working in the complaints department, a pleasant assignment since the company always stood firmly behind its policy of Goods Satisfactory or Money Refunded.

Eaton's was the department store that went to war, a tradition begun in 1885 when Timothy Eaton paid for the outfitting of employees who volunteered to fight Louis Riel during the Northwest Rebellion. When the Great War broke out in 1914, Jack Eaton, son of Timothy and then president of the company, vowed not only to continue paying salaries to volunteers, but to return to the government profits made on the sale of war materials as well. Jack Eaton was already celebrated as the first man in the Dominion to own an automobile (a White Steamer of twenty horsepower, Ontario plate No. 1) and as the builder of the country's first two-car garage, which he erected on a lot next to the family home of fifty rooms, fourteen bathrooms and a two-room hospital. Early in the Great War, which killed or wounded two men for every family in the country (which is perhaps why that war is still so much with us), Jack Eaton outfitted the Eaton Machine Gun Battery at his own expense, and dressed his young sons in officer's uniforms for official photographs. These patriotic gestures earned Jack a knighthood and allowed the Eaton family (as Sir John and Lady Flora) access to the British aristocracy, in whose company Lady Flora, once a country girl from Omemee, Ontario, would, by observing the table manners of the Duchess of Connaught, learn to eat a ripe peach with a knife and fork. "To move among royalty always gives me a special thrill," Lady Flora wrote in a chapter of her autobiography devoted to royal encounters ("honoured by a firm handclasp and friendly greeting by King George VI") and to a description of a diamond brooch she had had specially made in the Eaton's jewellery shop, and which was "admired and commented upon by both HM Queen Mary and HM Queen Elizabeth."

Before Lady Flora's time, Eaton's had been part of the culture of daily life in Canada for more than a generation, ever since the first mail order catalogues had gone out to the hinterland in the 1880s. Whole towns equipped themselves from the Eaton's catalogue, and one of them—Eatonia, in Saskatchewan—named itself after it. In 1888 you could order a complete kit of supplies for the Klondike gold rush; in 1901 you could order a two-storey house ready for assembly for the sum of $1,122.09. The Eaton's system of pricing (never round-dollar amounts) introduced the one-cent coin to Winnipeg, whose citizens, it is said, had, until Eaton's opened there in 1907, been reluctant to adopt it.

In 1921 my grandfather met the woman who would become my grandmother; she too was an Eaton's employee (of which there were now more than 10,000), a secretary in the administrative offices; perhaps they fell in love at one of the Eaton's picnics in Kildonan Park. When their first son, who would become my father, was old enough to take a part-time job in the late '30s, he too went to Eaton's, where he worked in the mail order building (which was as large as the store itself), assembling binder canvas for farmers who were not yet using combines to harvest their fields. There he was surrounded by men in white shirts who wore elastic garters on their biceps and sleeve protectors over their shirtcuffs. A kid named Jimmy Graham, who lived down the block, had the messenger job, and all through the shift Jimmy Graham rattled and rasped over the concrete floors on roller skates. In those days men wore hats, and my father remembers his father setting out every morning in a fedora and a suit. Later, when my father was in medical school, he worked as a clerk in Retail; he remembers his first Bargain Day, which took place during an August heat wave: the shrill ringing of the opening bell followed by an ominous rumble, and then a rolling thunder in the ceiling as the shoppers swept into the store and poured down the stairwells to the basement where my father and the other clerks, already perspiring in the heat, waited uneasily behind tables heaped with long underwear and other winter dry goods.

Eaton's was at the centre of genteel life in Winnipeg, as it was in Toronto (where for years a life-sized statue of Queen Victoria occupied the foyer in the main store): a place free of tobacco, playing cards and beverage alcohol. Near the main entrance sat the enormous bronze likeness of a dour man in a heavy suit, known familiarly as "Timothy's statue"—already to my parents' generation a relic of a distant age—and a good spot to meet up with friends. Every morning dozens of shiny blue and red delivery wagons left the Eaton's warehouse in military order, drawn by high-stepping horses clattering splendidly into the street before the crowd of onlookers that gathered every day to watch. On Sundays the merchandise displays in the windows along Portage Avenue were hidden away behind heavy drapes, a mute remonstrance to any who might be tempted to tarry on their way to church. When World War Two began my parents were teenagers, and in the last year of the war they met at the weekly military dance sponsored by the Eaton's Service Centre. They had both by this time appeared as models in Eaton's catalogues (did they recognize each other when they met?), as did many university students in the city: my mother in blouses and skirts (never in lingerie, she assures me), and my father in long underwear. Modelling for the catalogue paid well: a day's wage (five dollars) for a couple of hours' work. The catalogue was by then a literary and cultural resource, ranking in importance for many families with the works of Charles Dickens and the *Book of Knowledge*. In its pages one could find intelligence of the larger world, a hint of mild eroticism, and sturdy examples of unadorned English prose (superlatives were forbidden its pages: no products were claimed to be amazing, colossal, fabulous or perfect; language had first to be accurate: even "shrink resistant" could only be used with circumspection).

For most of this century, Eaton's has had a presence in Canadian life at least as great as any other institution—cultural, commercial or political—but that presence is almost never to be encountered in literature. By 1979, when Roch Carrier wrote *The Hockey Sweater*, 35,000 people were working for Eaton's, and (according to one of Timothy Eaton's biographers) twenty-five million children in North America watched the Eaton's Santa Claus parade that Christmas, most of them convinced that the Eaton's Santa was the only real Santa out there. The Eaton's catalogue plays a central role in *The Hockey Sweater* (the plot turns on the failure of the mail order department to include French-language order forms with its French-language catalogue), which is only twenty-four pages long and may be the only literary work we have that reflects the Eatonian fact at the heart of Canadian life. Where are the novels, the poems, the stories that one might expect such an empire to spawn?

Perhaps the reason lies with Timothy Eaton himself, founder and patriarch, known to his pious senior staff as "the Governor." Timothy Eaton was a tight-lipped man who distrusted notebooks and the people who wrote in them. He was an immigrant from Ulster who left school at thirteen and his country at eighteen. He appeared in Ottawa in 1854 and went to work on his brother's farm in Georgetown, where he adopted the Methodist faith, married a Methodist woman and sired three children. In 1869 he opened a dry goods store in Toronto, which he was determined to operate on the basis of One Fixed Price and the Cash System. His favourite drink was salted buttermilk.

Such are the materials of a life, but not perhaps of a stirring narrative. When he was a young man fresh from Ulster, his biographer tells us, he felled an unruly calf with a single blow (the calf recovered consciousness). When he was older he discouraged a dog from chasing his chickens by fixing a string of firecrackers to its tail. He was a man who "loved a regatta," but he detested men who sold insurance. He never attended a theatrical performance, although he devoted part of his fortune to the Margaret Eaton School of Literature and Expression, which was named for his wife, whose dream the school had been and whose motto was: We strive for the good, the true and the beautiful.

Timothy Eaton's favourite aphorism was "It's dogged as does it." He was overheard saying to one of his buyers: "Remember this—the greatest number of sticks and stones are found under the good apple trees." He commissioned a private printing of the Book of Proverbs, copies of which he pressed from time to time upon his managers—to one of whom he was overheard quoting verse 1:10 ("If sinners entice thee, consent thou not"). He never made a public speech, nor did he ever express a political opinion.

He offered his employees—whom he referred to as his "associates," or even "fellow associates"—a living wage and a measure of dignity in an age that often withheld both from working people who were everywhere else struggling for the eight-hour day, but at Eaton's had it bestowed upon them. In return he required absolute loyalty, and his descendants were assiduous strugglers against unions. He sponsored family picnics and at Christmas an enormous turkey dinner served, as Lady Flora put it, "on 50,000 pieces of china and cutlery." He was one of the first to employ women as buyers, but always maintained that women must keep one foot on the floor, "even when reaching for high packages." He performed a number of good deeds, but he never cracked a joke while anyone was listening. One of his biographers laments the lack of a Boswell for "Eaton's Johnson," but then what would Boswell have done with such a talker?

"I wish I had five hundred men who would mind their own business."

"Fill it with goods and sell them."

"Take the bus next time, George."

"I want my customers satisfied."

"Never talk business when eating."

"Keep the stock moving."

"Here—sit in that chair."

Timothy Eaton was a man who went to work. When he died in 1907 he had amassed five million dollars and nine thousand employees. His remains lie in an enormous mausoleum that resembles the Bank of Montreal. In literature his counterpart is Old Fezziwig in *A Christmas Carol*, who is shown to us by the Ghost of Christmas Past, feasting his employees on Christmas Eve. But where Fezziwig is garrulous, Eaton is silent; while Fezziwig dances through the night, Eaton sits stonily in his chair. Old Fezziwig in the Dickensian cosmos is the last of the family merchants, patriarch to family and employees; soon he will disappear from the Old World, pushed aside by numbers men like Scrooge and Marley. Old Timothy is the inversion of Fezziwig, but not his opposite: his is Christmas Yet to Come, here in the New World, where, steadfast and dour, he will become (as did we all, once?), a beginning of things and not an end.

THE MAN WHO STOLE
CHRISTMAS

O n a dark day in Toronto in January, when the sky was much too close to the ground, I went to see the grave of Timothy Eaton with my friend Walmsley. We wanted to memorialize our friend Brian Shein, who had first proposed Timothy Eaton as a cultural demiurge, and whose death a few years ago had cut short his ongoing study of the Eaton saga. I took a cab from my hotel over to where Walmsley was staying, and after a hearty lunch we swung out onto the sidewalk before a bitter following wind. I took my hands out of my pockets long enough to get my collar up and we made little quick steps down a long hill covered in ice to the subway station, where we turned in just as I was beginning to regret not having suitable boots. Walmsley handed me a token to put in the box and I slipped behind him through the rotating bars into the Paid Zone. We had gone down a set of concrete stairs and were moving out onto a platform covered in slippery yellow tiles when Walmsley said, have you any idea what a Great Attractor is? I did have an idea, a vague idea anyway, because I had been reading about chaos theory only a few weeks earlier. A train pulled in and we stepped inside, and I asked him where he'd heard about it. In the New York Times, he said, and I was surprised: I had no idea that Walmsley read the New York Times.

We found two seats facing forward and Walmsley said it was something about the Milky Way, which was falling into this Great

Attractor at four hundred miles a second. I tried to remember what I had read about Attractors. It seemed to me that they were more like relationships than actual things. Our train was hurtling forward by now, through a long tunnel. Walmsley said, what the hell is chaos theory?—and I had to admit that I couldn't quite get a handle on it. But it seemed to me that this news about the Milky Way ought to put the kibosh on the Big Bang Theory. What did we know about the Big Bang, really? You would have had to be there in that first one-millionth of a second. (The rest, of course, is entropy.) We mulled this over as the train decelerated, stopped, opened and closed its doors and pushed on again, pressing eastward beneath the freezing city. I remembered reading something somewhere about the Entropy Barrier, which is what stops us from going back in time: apparently entropy approaches infinity as you slow time down. Walmsley said, how would you do that anyway? The train continued its erratic haul, stopping and starting, as we leaned back and then forward, compensating for the Gs.

We left the train at Walmsley's signal and he led me into a crowded warren of escalators and hallways, talking over his shoulder as he led me up or down and around, along corridors filled with people moving rapidly with us or against us, finally out onto yet another platform sheathed in damp yellow tiles. All sense of direction had by now deserted me. A cold wind sucked in along the tunnel and another train pulled up in front of us. Walmsley was saying, you know what Hans Kung says about reincarnation: given one impossibility—the first birth—there is no reason not to accept another—a second birth, and so on. A few minutes later we were out on the sidewalk, bent into the wind, and I knew that I was completely lost. It's along here somewhere, Walmsley said, and we began working our way across and up sidehills, past the brick and glass facades of minor thoroughfares, until we came upon a hedged breach in one of them, and a low sign denoting the entrance to Mount Pleasant Cemetery.

As we entered the cemetery grounds along a narrow byway, the sounds of the city fell away, and we felt the temperature drop another notch. Before us white ground rose up to grey sky, all etched over by the skinny black skeletons of indeterminate trees hibernating like the low bushes, also black and leafless, that smudged the nearby snow. We were walking into the land of the dead, and soon we began to notice tombstones deposited here and there along the path. The road dropped down into a creek bottom and then forked at the base of a steep bluff. A wooden sign with diagrammatic markings on it poked up from the snow; when we reached it we found that it bore numbers only, no names, and that snow was stuck to our socks. The rich would have purchased the view, we reasoned, and so took the left fork up the hill. Off to one side a black marble block lay in the snow, one word engraved in its shiny surface: BLACK—a blunt, modernist touch. Then, as we gained the ridge, the larger crypts began to heave into view, first a series of modest eight- or nine-footers, then larger ones cast in a Grecian mode and bearing Anglo-Saxon names set into grey concrete. Everything was grey or white and the air was growing colder with each step we took. The Eaton crypt was by far the largest of the Greek temples; we glimpsed it first through a screen of gnarled black branches and knew it immediately to be what we were seeking. It was a squat, sullen version of the Parthenon, with heavy pillars and a pair of concrete Roman lions crouching by the stairs. To approach it we had to break trail through an expanse of crusted snow; by now my knees ached from the cold. The mausoleum was entirely grey, and bore chiselled into its upper facade a terse legend—E A T O N—in the familiar *sans serif* of the company logo. We could find no other epitaph; indeed, the company logo seemed to serve well enough, emblem of the Cash System and reminder to all who behold it that Honesty is the Best Policy, that no tobacco, liquor or playing cards are available on these premises.

Where was Shein now? All that remained of Timothy Eaton, at least, was right in front of us. Cautiously we mounted the icy steps of the crypt and peered into its dark interior through a tiny hole in a grille set into the main door. In the weak light we could make out a strip of carpet on a concrete floor, a large candelabrum and, set into the interior walls, an array of horizontal doors laid out in the manner of a lateral filing cabinet—twenty-two of them, harbouring, we presumed, the bones of the Eatonian generations. We were looking in upon the afterlife of Timothy Eaton and both of us were freezing. We made our withdrawal rapidly and without ceremony, shivering and blowing into our hands, and we slipped back down the hill into the city.

Back in the underground train we relaxed and rubbed our hands and began to speak again in lowered voices. There was something I was going to say, but then the train stopped and Walmsley leapt up and we disembarked into a stream of commuters carrying shopping bags and moving intently in several directions. Walmsley was talking over his shoulder again and I understood that he was expert at this; he talked and led me through the maelstrom of shoppers onto an escalator without jostling, and I realized that we were going up into the Eaton Centre and knew then what we were looking for. We're nearly there, said Walmsley. Just push on behind me.

We transited several departments—perfume, jewellery, men's wear—before reaching the statue, tucked up against a pillar near the main door: Timothy Eaton in bronze and, modestly, only slightly larger than life, set stiffly into a straight-backed chair with his hands on his knees, one foot in front of the other, every inch the thrifty Methodist merchant. His chair stood on a pedestal about three feet high; a dirty green rust covered him and the chair completely, save for the toe of his left shoe, which extended forward slightly, and which gleamed metallic yellow in the fluorescent light. The toe was the only thing about him that might be said to give off light; it glowed warmly before us: I reached out—as had myriad customers before me seeking Shopper's Luck—and let my fingers rest there on the cold bronze toe of the monument. When I got home a few days later I pulled out a letter from Shein written ten years earlier, to which he had added the following postscript:

Must tell you that, using map and calliper, I spent an afternoon last week determining the precise centre of Canada. It is 43 deg 39' 22 1/2" North by 79 deg. 23' 00" West and about 83 metres above sea level. This is the still unturning point from which rises the greenish-black marble supporting the statue of Timothy E., the Man Who Stole Christmas, Born 1834—Died $5,000,000.

ANOTHER COUNTRY

Twenty-five years ago there was no speed limit in that country where tiny white crosses sprouted from the side of the highway, and you drank whiskey by the shot with a beer chaser; there was a way of grasping your cigarette that implied great significance in that country, and a way of hunkering down in order to draw a picture in the dirt when you had something to say. I used to drive borrowed cars along the secondary highways into that country, or sometimes I would ride the Greyhound down to Seattle and take the train overnight across the Rocky Mountains. The coffee in that country was always bad, and the worst coffee was train coffee, which was triumphantly bad as I recall it. This was Montana, home of my mentor and friend Roger, whom I used to visit whenever I could; now that I am old and have a car of my own and they have speed limits in that country, I seem never to go there any more.

The second-last time I went down to that country, Roger called me up and said he had been given a map written on the back of an envelope which showed how to get to an enormous boulder covered in petroglyphs that lay miles off the roadway on the prairie up by the Alberta border. Roger wanted to go and find that boulder; so a few days later we set out from Missoula in a north-easterly direction in Roger's Toyota pickup with a mini-camper strapped on, and with a couple of fishing rods, a cooler full of beer and a bag of beef jerky, and stopped late in the afternoon beside a lake jumping with fish. I had learned how to cast spinners and flies working in the Hudson's Bay Sporting Goods in 1969 (I could put a fly on the right-hand corner of the underwear table which was deep in Men's Wear), but this was the first chance I had to do that kind of fishing outdoors, and I had four tiny bass landed within about twenty minutes. Cleaning them was less pleasant, but when the sun went down we had them frying slowly over the fire in a half pound of butter. Roger, whose store of wilderness lore was greater than mine (hence the beer, the jerky and a bag of groceries), proved to be not much of a fish man, and I did most of the eating. I recall taking very small bites, nibbles really, and washing them down with plenty of beer.

Next day we hit the open plain, which was dry and hot and broken every few miles by broad stretches of asphalt and heavy wire fencing: they were underground silos, with their missiles pointed at Russia. This was Ground Zero country; Roger said when we got onto Indian land we'd be out of it. Ours was the only vehicle in sight. Soon we were approaching the Missouri River, which I had not known to be in this country; I had thought it was farther east, Kentucky perhaps, or Virginia: folksong country. We stopped for gas and the woman in the store warned us to watch our backs if we were going to Indian country, where they were "murdering and stabbing each other every night," she said. We camped at the edge of the Missouri and Roger threw together a goulash dinner after I had made a few unsuccessful casts into the swiftly flowing waters.

In the morning we pulled into a little town on the Indian reservation and the first thing I noticed was the absence of corpses on its few gravel roads. (I had laughed at the woman in the store but her words had frightened me.) We stocked up on more groceries and wandered around for a while, and by mid-afternoon we were off the highway and rolling over bald prairie along a faint track that ran on and on over the folding ground ahead of us. The sky was a huge blue dome and there were no clouds, and for the next twenty-four hours we saw no other human beings. Small antelope began to appear in the distance, and jackrabbits with black and white ears bounced away from us like deer. Prairie hens scurried into the sage and flurries of yellow-breasted meadowlarks shot straight into the sky. We could feel the wind now, and when we got out to stretch, it swept over us like rushing water. We stopped for lunch in a creek bottom where there were small trees and cattle looking for a drink. The only way to understand this kind of country was to walk on it, feel it swelling incessantly and crunching underfoot, see the horizon shifting crazily every few steps. I watched Roger half a mile away standing upright on the crest of a swell; he moved downhill toward me and disappeared into the folding land, to reappear again and then again, and I could never predict where.

We found the boulder where the map had said it would be, an enormous flat rock ten feet across, three feet high, covered in carvings and surrounded by a white picket fence. The fence seemed entirely appropriate, even out here in what seemed to be the middle of nowhere. We were standing on a broad plateau and the wind beat against us ferociously; we had to turn away from it to speak. We camped at the lip of a coulee where there were many tepee rings, circles of small boulders, some of them smoothed and shaped and bearing the marks of the people who had worked them. As it grew dark I felt that we were accompanied in that place. Later it began to rain and the wind knocked the Toyota back and forth on its springs.

We began our return to Missoula by driving west along the Canadian border. There were clouds in the sky now and the air shimmered around us and the wind never stopped. In the afternoon we came to the battleground on which the Nez Percé with Chief Joseph met their final defeat. It was a beautiful creek bottom that opened up abruptly onto the flat plain over which the U.S. Army advanced a hundred and twenty years ago, putting an end to the thousand-mile march of the Nez Percé toward Canada and sanctuary. Pathways running through the site took us past brass markers on which were named the dead of that day, Native and soldier alike; other markers indicated where each tepee had been, and the names of the families that had occupied them. The cannon had fired down into the camp from the edge of the plain. On one bluff stood a recently-erected monument to the war chief Looking Glass and those who died on that spot with him. The battleground had been marked out hours after the battle by a local farmer who must have apprehended the significance of what had transpired here. Roger and I were the only ones there that afternoon. Down at the creek there was no wind; we climbed to the plateau and the wind scoured our faces as we looked north toward Canada, thirty miles away. We traversed the site in several directions and studied the markers as if they might yield meaning to us. I became aware of a litter of cigarette butts lying everywhere in the short grass; it seemed an irreverence that people would put out their cigarettes on such ground. Then I saw that none of the cigarettes appeared to have been lit; they had been dropped whole on the ground and left there to decay and to turn a dirty brown. It was offensive to me, and when I saw fresh unstained cigarettes on the ground that must have been dropped there earlier in the day, I remarked aloud on the unsightliness. Roger told me then that these were tobacco offerings, gifts of memory, and tears stood out in my eyes as I began to understand where I was. I opened my pack of Players and took out a cigarette to drop upon the ground.

TALES OF THE CITY

LAWN VITÉ

In the restaurant in Montreal a drunken publisher from Newfoundland was determined to sing in a loud voice all of the stanzas of a lengthy and beautiful sea shanty written by Stan Rogers, but an editor from Vancouver and a poet from Saskatoon, both of whom were also drunk, kept interrupting him by singing impromptu fragments of a cruder and less beautiful sea shanty, the first line of which could be repeated easily with simple variations: "O my name is John O'Riley and I sail upon the sea." With each interruption, the publisher from Newfoundland began again at the beginning of the sea shanty written by Stan Rogers and then the editor and the poet broke in with more iambic verses ending with the sound of the long *e* as they were able to make them up. This went on for some time, until certain of the well-proportioned men and women in black and white clothing who worked in the restaurant began to utter threats and imprecations in the language of the Québécois, and at last the publisher from Newfoundland was allowed to proceed uninterrupted from beginning to end. After the deep silence that followed the last line of the last chorus, which begins "I'm a broken man on a Halifax pier," everyone in the restaurant applauded, and it was never clear whether they were applauding the singer, the song or the silence, which seemed, as I recall it, to be saturated with relief.

The occasion was a literary dinner and the name of the restaurant was the Lawn Vité, a name I had taken to be a bilingual play on words meaning something like "the lively lawn," and it made me want to love Montreal for its legendary cosmopolitanism. We were sitting at many small tables pulled together and I remember thinking that one rarely sees a crowd of publishers and writers entertaining each other so well, although by that time I had consumed enough wine to render my perceptions unreliable. Eventually we settled our accounts and dispersed into the night. At five o'clock in the morning the man with whom I was staying, who was a historian of the fur trade and an old friend, awoke suddenly with the unhappy conviction that he had written a forty-dollar tip onto his hundred-dollar invoice at the Lawn Vité. He got out of bed and found the receipt in his wallet and brought it out into the living room where his wife and I were waiting for the sun to come up while continuing the high-level talks that had begun at the literary dinner. My friend showed us the receipt and indeed, the tip he had written in on the appropriate line was for forty dollars, and there was nothing to do but console him for his mistake. A mistake of my own became clear at the same moment, when I perceived the name of the restaurant as imprinted on the receipt to be *L'invitée* and not what I had so happily understood it to be until that moment.

Some years later, after my friend the historian and his family had moved away from Montreal, he told me that he had been back to L'invitée many times, and that each time he had shaved off a dollar or two from the tip until reaching an acceptable balance. After that he went there no more, not because of the cookery or the service, which were top-notch, but because the walls of L'invitée were painted a hideous shade of pink that caused him pain every time he laid eyes upon it. This threw me into further confusion, because in my memory of the literary dinner, the walls of the Lawn Vité had been painted a particular shade of deep green known to colourists as Bohemian Green Earth.

HEAT

It was the first hot day of summer and the bus was full up with people trying not to sweat too much; the air in the bus was heavy and sluggish and conversations were muffled by the heat and the whine and groan of the electric engine stopping and starting, stopping and starting, flattening out time and life as it hauled us slowly forward to our separate destinations. Then a voice materialized in the din, as a woman at the back of the bus said in a clear, confident tenor: "I cried like a baby when he said he was getting a sex change on the telephone." In an instant everyone on the bus became alert. I put down my book and pulled a note card from my shirt pocket, and the guy next to me and the kid on his knee watched as I wrote down the sentence that seemed still to be resonating in my ears. "I cried like a baby when he said he was getting a sex change on the telephone." I wasn't sure where to put the punctuation. Then the voice spoke again, and the woman said: "His wife was a fat cow like I am, that bovine bitch." I wrote that down too. Only the kid turned around to see who was speaking.

Now everyone on the bus was paying attention to the woman at the back. She seemed to be talking to a companion, but her tone suggested that she was speaking to each of us separately. "I always wanted to be a doctor, you understand, but what I really am is a witch doctor," she said. "He cried like a baby, and what could I do?" I wanted to turn around and look at her but I wasn't ready to risk making eye contact. She said: "My brothers are all doctors and lawyers and police officers; I wanted to be a doctor too, but with the psychological guerrilla warfare these days, you know what I mean."

The bus continued its passage through the city. I waited with my note card for the woman to speak again, and when she did I forgot to keep writing. I had gotten lost on a train of thought. When I heard her again, the guy next to me and the kid had disappeared, and the woman was saying, "and then they started that cloning in 1932, this is the fact of it, when Einstein was around, I swear to God I'm related. When you see Billy tell him I got a nose job in case he doesn't recognize me, but I still believe totally in sports. Everyone should do sports, especially gymnastics." The bus had come to a stop and then started again, and now the voice was silent. Up behind the driver four kids facing each other on the benches were making shapes in the air with their fingers: they were speaking to each other in the language of the deaf. I watched them for a while, unable to comprehend anything they were saying, and then got up and went to the door as the bus came to my stop. I looked down to the rear of the bus and there were three women sitting apart from each other at the back. None of them was speaking. As I stepped down from the bus a man about sixty years old strode past; he was portly and balding and his hands were tucked into the pockets of a lightweight windbreaker. He was leaning forward and saying to a much younger man: "So I slipped the guy a G-note, you know what I mean?" He looked exactly like a mobster in a Mafia movie. I paused and watched him walk down the street with his elbows stuck out. It was the first hot day of summer, and it was much too hot to think.

When the heat comes to the west coast, the sky turns a searing red at sundown and stays that way long into the evening. The effect is spectacular, but not pleasant, and as long as the red is in the sky it remains too hot to think. The thinking comes later, when a cooling breeze draws people into the streets, and we pass each other strolling along the avenue, peering into cafes and restaurants, contemplating nothing more than the pleasing lateness of the hour.

Stepping out to the corner store after midnight becomes a privilege, a chance to partake in wisdom, in the promise of late summer nights past, when we used to ask ourselves: shall we be kind, shall we be wise? In the corner store the air is filled with the racket of refrigerators pumping heat into the room to keep the soft drinks cool. The clerk sits listlessly by the fan; he looks like he's melting. I leave him a tip, which makes him smile, and then I escape back into the warm, liberating night.

I came under the spell of warm nights with friends who were as old as I was when I was young and desired the world; only in those warm late nights in the city was it possible to speak of such things. Then were the hours full of promise, and desire; and meaning lay everywhere within reach. We went into bars and cafes, we observed the young men in automobiles who cruised up and down the street without ceasing, their elbows thrust significantly from open windows: they were the tragic, the lost in the night. We, on the other hand, were the found: we were unafraid of talk, and at least we had found each other. And we too wished the night to last forever, or at least until the promise was fulfilled.

Now in mid-August the heat wave is upon us, and I write with the doors and windows open in the middle of the night; outside the streets are filled with garbage as the strike wears on, and the city has come to resemble New York in the photographs and movies that present garbage as a signifier of Big City life, so no one is bothered by garbage any more: we go out in the night and step easily through the trash along the avenue. Once I went to Toronto in August during a heat wave and observed people folding up in the heat like concertinas on the kerbs and on the stairs of office buildings. Toronto was the epitome of big city heat, which I could feel as a heavy weight pressing down upon me as I stepped off the airport bus and a rain of sweat erupted over all of my body. Within moments I was blinded by sweat, and all that passed in that day occurred through a hallucinatory screen. I had an address to find and a map, and there were yellow taxis everywhere, but when I approached one it turned out to be a police car, and it seemed an unkindness to me to paint police cars the colour of taxis. I determined to walk to where I had to go, and I walked for many hours through streets heaped with trash and thronging with people much better dressed than I was; from time to time the crowd would part, as one of its members sank to the ground. Near street corners large signs on poles said No Standing and threatened offenders with a heavy fine; here was further unkindness, for I took this to be part of an anti-vagrancy program and whenever one of these signs appeared I was careful to keep moving, however slowly, with one eye peeled for yellow cars. I remember looking up at the sky, which seemed unusually far away and contained no clouds, but the sky was not blue; it had been bleached nearly white and it hurt my eyes to look at it. I was alone in a big city and it was against the law to stand still; I could expect no less but to keep moving, like an exhausted swimmer drowning in heat at the farthest end of the earth.

Heat reminds us always of itself: is it as hot now as it was then? we ask ourselves. No doubt there comes a time when the hottest days are all in the past: we will never see heat like that again, we say, but how can we know that? Two weeks ago a storm erupted over the city, and for most of the afternoon forks of lightning shot down onto tall buildings and thunder smashed open the air over our heads and sirens screamed throughout the city. When the storm passed, the heat returned, and we knew that such a storm, the likes of which had never been seen before in these parts, would never come again, in the afternoon, during a heat wave.

SNOW

We left town in a bus two days before Christmas, in the late afternoon, as the city filled up with snow. The bus depot was crowded with grim travellers clutching boxes and bundles and too many suitcases; some were overdressed in parkas and snowboots; many were accompanied by small overdressed children; all were determined not to panic. Could there ever be enough buses for all of us? Outside on the platform we shuffled into place at the end of a long line with our bundles and parcels and recited our destination to a series of intense young men in blue jackets who patrolled up and down asking everyone the same question and looking us in the eye as if to convince us that things were going to be all right. We could see the snow falling in big lazy flakes, into the vault of bright fluorescent light that washed over the paved yards and the big blue buses that would carry us away, out of the city and through the storm.

Our driver had fine white hair, which he wore swept high in a pompadour. He was about my age, but slender, and completely unperturbed. (I hadn't seen one of those haircuts since I was a kid.) He smiled as he tore off our tickets and waved us aboard. Finally he hopped in and slung the door shut and rolled us out onto the muffled streets of a city that seemed no longer to be ours, now that we were seeing it through smoked glass and a further screen of falling snow. In moments we had made our way out of the neighbourhood of dingy beer parlour hotels and were moving over the viaduct between two domed stadiums lit up with golfball lights, toward the steel and glass core of the city. The Santa Claus in front of the Bay was playing an electric guitar under the overhang. He had on those gloves with no fingers and his uniform was too big, and he looked cold and rather desperate, but that might have been because we couldn't hear his music inside the bus, where the only sounds were the low murmur of voices and the growl of the big diesel engine. The windows were damp with condensation and we had to wipe them with our hands to see outside. It was warm in the bus and soon people were taking off their coats and standing up to put them in the overhead rack.

In the big park at the edge of the city the grassy lawns were covered in snow, and the trees, always so dark and so green, were white too. As we sped through the park no one spoke. When we got to the ferry dock it was dark and a gusting wind blew the snowflakes fiercely into the tinted window glass. The driver switched off the engine and we sat in silence as vehicles moved slowly along the concrete on either side of us and shadowy men in fluorescent orange vests gestured them into position. Off to the left, in a pool of harsh industrial light, waiting foot passengers clustered in the mouth of a sheltered walkway. I felt like a child observing the mysterious, ominous procedures of the larger world. Riding on trains, or in the back seat of my parents' station wagon, travelling in winter: always the world outside in motion, enacting processes beyond a child's comprehension, punctuated at points of arrival or departure by the sounds of machinery and the elusive murmur of strangers. At these moments all is uncertainty and crisis, and imminent loss; and the question no one asks aloud: Will we ever see home again?

That question is weighted with an emotion that must be older than I am. I presume this because I felt it years before encountering those images, usually (especially) black-and-white, of refugees crowded onto platforms, of imprisoned families crowded into stockades, that coloured my sense of dislocation even now as the bus rolled into the bright empty maw of the ferry's belly: clang, clang, over the metal ramp, the dull bleat of invisible foghorns sounding in the distance.

An hour later, on the other shore, the highway was soon reduced to black tracks in the snow and then the tracks began to disappear and the road ahead was completely white and we were advancing into a vortex of swirling flakes. From time to time the bus slowed to a stop and people got off in ones or twos, to disappear into the blasted night. Now there was silence again in the bus and we were straining to peer forward past the white head of our driver and into the blizzard as the bus dropped into low gear for the hills and then up a gear for the downgrade. We were drifting up and around and down in a featureless world from which mere visibility seemed to have been erased. How could the driver know where we were going? In the beam of the headlights an impenetrable whirlwind danced a few feet ahead of us. Occasionally the red glow of taillights would materialize in that tiny space and the driver, determined to maintain our momentum, would gear down and pull out to pass. Only once did he falter in this manoeuvre, and then the bus lurched violently onto the shoulder and back into the roadway. There had been something in the way, he called out, an abandoned car. No one breathed for a moment and then people began applauding the driver. We were frightened in the snow, we were in danger, and only the driver could bring us through.

Now there were no other vehicles on the road and as we pressed into the night, I felt wash over me an emotion made up of trepidation and excitement and I was certain that everyone else was feeling it. (Would we ever see home again?) I looked around the shadowy interior at my fellow passengers and they seemed all to be concentrating on the same thing, eyes forward, heads up, helping the driver keep the bus on the road, as the snow fell heavily; in the beam of the headlights the snow flew straight toward us, and seemed to sweep us endlessly into itself, pulling us into its source, and away from home.

GRAND CASINO

The Grand Casino convenes 364 nights a year in a room upstairs at the Blue Boy Hotel at the south end of Vancouver near the suburbs. The doors open at six p.m. and the action proceeds for ten hours straight, a period of time that seems not so much to flow as to hang suspended between adjacent points on the continuum: gambling makes its own time in rooms like this one, with strips of tiny beaded lights running along the walls, dark carpets, pools of light over the gambling tables, and everywhere the ceaseless murmur of Muzak like a nascent headache waiting to be born. Soon the Muzak is subsumed in the persistent rustle of plastic chips falling softly one onto another as the players pick them up in little stacks and let them fall one at a time through their fingers. This is the fundamental gesture in the Grand Casino: those sitting down let their chips fall onto the table; those standing let them fall from hand to hand, and soon the sound of chips falling and falling again fills the air like the steady rush of water in a creek. Eventually the room is full of people, perched on high stools at the card tables, leaning over roulette wheels and strolling among the tables (there are nineteen tables in the Grand Casino) waiting for the hunch, the whim that will set them betting again.

Nothing here is like it is in the movies. There is no alcohol, for one thing, which may be why there is no sense of tension building up in the room. Everything proceeds at an unwavering pace. Cards fall, wheels spin, the dealers rake up the chips with their hands. Refreshments can be obtained from the low-grade snack bar set into one wall: Coca Cola in cans seems to be the favourite drink; potato chips in bags the favourite snack. There is a disarming rec-room aspect to the Grand Casino; people here wear rec-room clothing, eat rec-room food. The chief of security is a tall grand-father man with grey hair at his temples; he wears a tan sports jacket and looks like Dashiell Hammett must have looked: sea-soned, a touch world-weary, but kind, a kind-looking man; he has a slight stoop, the result no doubt of decades of lending an ear to shorter, more inept people like me and my friends from the non-profit society which will share in the evening's profits. When the chief of security talks to you, you feel like you're being let in on the know. He escorts the big winners out the back way to the parking lot and waits for them to drive away safely. His assistant is a young muscular man who handles ID-checks and writes poetry in the daytime; he says he wants to write a novel before his thirtieth birthday.

Everyone in the Grand Casino wears a poker face, which is the human face of the evening: nothing can be read there. Young and old, men and women—it is impossible to determine who is win-ning or losing. Friends smile at each other; people whisper in each other's ears and give nothing away. Everyone stands on their dignity. At the roulette tables crowds of players form and dissipate like clouds in the sky, clustering at one table, piling enormous stacks of chips all over the board, and then suddenly breaking up and coalescing at other tables. At one of the roulette tables a young man sits on a stool (everyone else stands): he has a loose-leaf notebook on his lap and for at least an hour he has been writing down the winning numbers. By the time I get over to watch, he has begun to bet, a few chips at a time, first looking through his list of numbers and then putting down the bet. He loses every time.

One of the dealers says the man is there every night working on his system, and every night he loses. At the one-dollar blackjack tables a tiny ancient grandmother in slippers seems to be well known to everyone. She too is a regular, as are many of the people here, for whom gambling seems not to be a mystery, and for whom the Grand Casino is the most ordinary of places.

At the blackjack tables the dealers distribute cards with a delicate flourish, turning their hands palms up like dancers at the completion of every action. All of the dealers' hands look the same as they float above the tables, but the dealers themselves are of every variety: heavy, light, tall and short, men and women wearing black trousers and white shirts. Every quarter hour they shift stations while making no interruption in the action, and they take short breaks in a private room at the side; there is no dinner break. One of them tells me the wages are low but the tips are high, and that the graceful turning-up of the palms is a gesture directed at the video cameras in the ceiling. For everything in the Grand Casino is under surveillance: the ceiling is studded with lenses and the cameras never stop running. (Later, when we count the take, the pit boss will hold each newly opened money box up to the ceiling after dumping its contents on the table.)

The evening wears on and the murmur of many conversations melts into the ambient sound of rushing water; I hear Asian languages and languages from Europe and Africa, and not much of the English language; this too is unlike the gambling world that I have seen in movies. Other-worldliness seems (to me) to pervade space and time in this place which opens for business every day but one. I am an outsider in the Grand Casino, along with my colleagues from the non-profit society which will benefit from the evening's action. When the play stops, the sound of rushing water recedes, and then there is only the Muzak. Now begins the counting of money in tiny windowless rooms behind two sets of locked doors, beneath the cameras in the ceilings. We stack and count the stacks and push them into counting machines and then count them again, until all the money has been counted and recounted, and then with a flourish we apply our signatures to documents, and the unlocking of the doors begins.

Outside in the languorous early morning, a few cars pass in the street; the neon glows above our heads. The people of the Grand Casino have long since dispersed into the metropolis. Later this evening they will gather again, without us.

AFTER THE WAR

For years I was a man with an enemy, although few who know me knew this about me, for having an enemy is not something one speaks about openly: this I began to realize after it was all over. My enemy, whose name was Bill, was an absurd tall man with wild hair and a stringy beard; he resembled a prophet in the Old Testament and he was not unaware of the effect. We had been friends for years before the enmity commenced, late one night in February of 1982, in his apartment, which was on the floor above mine in an old house that we owned with other friends. Bill had summoned me peremptorily by telephone, which was not how we usually communicated in that house, so I was in a manner of speaking forewarned of the unpleasantness to come; I filled a glass with whiskey and took it with me up the stairs to the landing in front of Bill's place, where it was hot and dry and always dark (the bulb had burned out three years earlier and had never been replaced). The door to Bill's apartment was ajar but I knocked anyway, and his command to enter issued instantly from within. Then I stepped from the dark into Bill's domain.

The man who would become my enemy was a dealer in old and rare books, and a collector of Canadian first editions during a period in which new Canadian writing was held in contempt by booksellers, academics and reviewers alike; I was a publisher of such new writing, and Bill's shop was one of the few places in the country where books like the ones I published could be found. I was drawn to him immediately at our first meeting, when he launched into a spectacular oration against the blockheads, the dolts and the swine who were wrecking the intellectual life of the country. This was the most literary of occasions: I had come with an armload of books into a dark room filled with high shelves crammed with books, and the air was filled with dust motes and the tang of old paper and musty bindings; I could feel a sneeze building up in my sinuses, but it never came. Boxes filled with books lay on the floor, and stacks of books were heaped up on a desk at the far end of the room, at which a tall bony man in a tweed jacket sat bashing away on an old Remington typewriter. He paused to look up at me and I felt myself rather ludicrously fixed to the spot, like the wedding guest in *The Rime of the Ancient Mariner*. He wore glasses with thick black frames and his small face seemed to recede from the bush of black hair surrounding it. He thrust out a hand with a flourish and said, in a way that he had of capitalizing certain words as he spoke: "Ah, yes. I have been Waiting for You." Then he began the oration against blockheads.

My friendship with Bill lasted nine years, and so did the oration, which he continued to elaborate, and which seemed so well to express a necessary anger shared by many who wished to make literature during that epoch. When I met him he was already known as a daunting figure on the fringe of the literary world, a source of imprecation and prophecy. One did not meet Bill so much as discover him: he was like a piece of geography. Writers and publishers visiting the city would make their way to his shop, always at their own peril, in order to experience the phenomenon they had heard about, and often they would emerge bruised and shaken by the force of his rhetoric and the terrible understanding that they too were to be counted among the blockheads. For one could never be certain that one was on the right side with Bill; and as the oration became more complex (and perhaps more desperate), more and more of us became ensnared by it.

At the time he seemed to be exactly what we needed: a master of the literary harangue, a magnificent ranter. He once told me that he had developed his style of declamation when he was a young man in Saskatchewan, by studying the recordings of Mort Sahl, the American comedian and virtuoso of the improvisational technique, whose signature remark was: "Is there anyone here I haven't offended?" Bill was magnificent in world-weariness as well, and when he appeared in the bar at night he would throw himself into a chair and heave a sigh that portended nothing more than the vast emptiness of the world. Sometimes he would smile benevolently and bestow kindness on the company. Such meetings were always brief, and I cannot recall more than once or twice having an extended conversation with him. He gave me the books of John Berger, which opened the world to me in a way that no other writing had ever done, but we never talked about Berger's ideas; Bill belonged more to the eighteenth century than to this one, to the age of *The Dunciad* and the angry balladeers of Grub Street. He took me with him to the Antiquarian Book Fair in San Francisco, where I became aware of a difference between who I was and who he wished me to be: he presented me to his colleagues as an exhibit from another world, perhaps even as a specimen of the non-blockhead, but I was awkward and dull and I disappointed him; his colleagues were as alien to me as I was to them, and I became forlorn during the dinner cruise, trapped in a phantasmagoric crowd of antiquarians endlessly circling Alcatraz Island.

He was profoundly unapproachable as I think of him now; he seemed outwardly to live an ascetic life, or at least an austere one. When he moved into his place in the house we shared, he ordered a full set of kitchen cabinets from Ikea, and then never cooked a meal at home; his furnishings were leftover ragged sofas and stuffed chairs that might have been retrieved from his time as a militant graduate student in the political science department, a career which ended abruptly when the police attacked and he was banned forever from the campus. One afternoon sounds of violence and cries of pain were heard emanating from his apartment, but he refused to be rescued when we went up the stairs: Just Go Away, he said, through the closed door, and later that night a woman in a long coat and stiletto heels was observed leaving the building and entering a cab. None of us mentioned the incident again. When a reporter wrote unkindly of him in the local paper, he shaved off his beard and cut his hair, with the result that he lost all outward aspect and with it most of his self-confidence, neither of which was regained until he had grown all his hair back and restored to himself (and to his friends) the figure of the bearded seer.

For some time before the night in 1982 when he summoned me to his apartment, I had noticed in Bill's oration a tendency to include me among those whom he was lately naming as block-heads, or perhaps I should say I could detect a likelihood that I was about to be so named. Certainly my thinking about the world had begun to diverge from his, and I wondered if the time had come to talk about it. He began by denouncing a number of my friends, whose influence upon me he described as repugnant, and then proceeded to the demand that I drop these people from my life. I waited for him to denounce me directly, but he never did. Instead he talked on and on against my friends, building slander upon slander, until he was incandescent with rage. I could feel him reaching into my life and trying to take hold of it, and I could feel my defences closing all the doors. Eventually he paused and I said that I would never engage in such a ludicrous exchange, and he said: "then I am your Enemy, and I will Block you." Even in my dismay I knew all of it to be ridiculous, a figment of melodrama, a scene in a bad novel. I picked up my glass (which must have been empty by then) and left Bill's apartment, and never entered it again.

In this way I became a man with an enemy. Some days passed before my revised status in the world began to take effect, when a close friend appeared in my doorway in tears. He had been to see Bill and had heard what he said were terrible things about me. He wanted to know what I was going to do and I had to tell him that I was going to do nothing. This scene was repeated with other friends, and I could feel Bill's hand in my life as he dispensed pain to my friends. Then there was silence. He sold out his share in the house and moved away without my laying eyes upon him. The years passed and I heard news of him from people who seemed not to know of what had transpired between us, although I could never be sure that they weren't just being polite. He began writing pamphlets against the literary world which were painful for me to read, and making public speeches which I never attended. His polemic began to incorporate a rhetoric of increasing violence, with much reference to hit lists and war criminals and close knife-fighting, and he took to describing himself as a man of war, at war.

I never learned to comport myself as a man with an enemy, a state of being for which there is no word in the dictionary. Having never pronounced myself my enemy's enemy, I had no real place in the relationship of enmity that Bill had defined for us. This was unsettling in an obscure way, and many months would pass without my thinking of it, until someone mentioned his name or an old memory surfaced unbidden from the shadows. Then self-consciousness would overcome me and I would feel like a character in a Graham Greene novel, a man in an overcoat pursued by the obscure consequences of some prior affinity gone wrong. It was a purely literary sensation.

And then I heard that Bill was moving to Russia. This was a few years after the Berlin Wall came down, and the story was that Bill was selling off his stock and leaving the country. I wondered whether I should be relieved at this news, which seemed to belong more to fiction than to reality: would this have any effect on my state of nonbeing? More years passed, and as rumours of Bill's life in Moscow came to my ears, I imagined him in that foreign place, always my enemy, holding forth in another language.

Then, not long ago, at a book fair in Vancouver, I learned that Bill had died the night before, in Victoria. Several people told me this, and each time I felt my face become a mask as I contemplated the absurd news that my enemy was no more. What response could I make? I said that I hadn't known he was back in the country. Later in the day a young woman said to me: who is this man who died that everyone is talking about?—and I heard myself laugh. Then I knew what I needed to say. I looked directly into her eyes and said: that man who died was my enemy for a very long time.

TALES OF THE CITY

Early in the summer a police spokeswoman came on the radio during the evening news to report a hostage-taking story. She spoke in the deadpan manner of official spokespersons, who often have to struggle to keep their stories from getting away from them. I got out my pen and began writing the story down as she was telling it. I had to write quickly; my transcription may not be wholly accurate, but I tried to preserve the particular diction of the police report.

She began by saying that an incident had occurred on the previous night when a citizen passing by a drugstore at the south end of Oak Street looked through the window and noticed people lying on the floor inside the store. The citizen also noticed a man wielding a gun standing over the people lying on the floor. There was another alleged person in the drugstore as well, she said.

The citizen who had looked into the drugstore window proceeded to call 911 from a pay phone, and the suspect, or possibly two suspects, rushed from the store and drove off in a vehicle with stolen Alberta plates, although the vehicle itself was not stolen. Within minutes police vehicles answering the 911 were in pursuit and soon they had the suspect or suspects surrounded in the 4000-block of Granville Street. At this point the suspect began ramming the police vehicles with his vehicle and then the suspect got out of his vehicle holding the gun in one hand and a two-and-a-half-month-old baby in the other hand. The police officers had their weapons out in response to the suspect being armed. The suspect entered one of the police vehicles and drove up Granville Street and the police gave chase. At this point there were thirty police officers involved in the incident. The suspect then smashed up the police vehicle at 22nd and Granville and jumped out with the baby and the gun and ran over to a black Jetta, whereupon the suspect pointed the gun at the woman driver of the black Jetta. But after looking into the Jetta the suspect decided he didn't want that vehicle and he went over to a van and forced the driver out of it. Then the suspect drove off in the van and the police gave chase. At this point the suspect still had the baby in one hand and the gun in the other, as the spokeswoman on the radio put it, and so it's not surprising that the suspect wasn't able to control the van. The van went onto the meridian and flipped. The suspect climbed out of the van with the baby and the gun and then realized that he had no ammunition in the gun, and the suspect was apprehended at that point. The spokeswoman paused, and then she said: trauma counsellors have been called in and they are now treating the thirty police officers, who have never seen anything like this in any of their careers.

A few weeks later I was reminded of the story of the man with the baby by a story in the paper (Test Sheds New Light on 1947 Park Murder Case), which opened with the statement that "new DNA evidence has changed the focus of the investigation into the Babes in the Woods murders of two children in Stanley Park half a century ago." "The babes" were thought until recently to be a boy and girl, but DNA tests now showed that they were both boys. The remains of the children were found near Beaver Lake on January 14, 1953: "It is believed the children were bludgeoned to death by a hatchet in 1947." After the case "lay dormant for several years," a police sergeant "came across the children's remains in the police museum." The sergeant decided "it was about time those kids were buried." So, he said, "I took samples out to Dr. David Sweet at UBC and had a service at sea." Then the story jumped from the police sergeant to the DNA doctor at the university, who said: "It's the identification of the victim that starts the investigation. It's not until you know who it is that you can start to look at the circumstances of the last known acquaintances or anything that would be relative to the case, like a disappearance." So now that the victims had been identified as boys, the police were sifting through three boxes of old files looking for clues. One clue was from "a teacher named Smith, who stated that he had seen a hysterical woman with blood on her shoes together with a nervous man in Stanley Park in 1947." Another clue was a tip from a man who reported that "a couple who had lived with him in a rooming house in the downtown area had two boys who disappeared." No other clues were given in the story, which wrapped up quickly with a reference to seven hundred unsolved murder cases in the province "dating to 1921," and the information that "DNA has been used to help identify the remains of the last czar in Russia and Jesse James in the United States."

In another story in the paper (Bank Ordered to Pay After Account Error), a judge ordered the Royal Bank to pay a young man $23,000 after a bank employee made a mistake that allowed the young man's partner in a diving business to clean out their joint bank account. The next paragraph reported that the young man had gone to the bank and opened a joint account requiring two signatures for withdrawals of money. But a Royal Bank employee had failed to check off a box on the signature card and, by making this mistake, allowed either party to withdraw funds. The rest of the story unfolded rapidly in tiny paragraphs, as follows:

The young man's partner, referred to only as Mr. Driussi of Kelowna, took out $23,000.

The young man, 26, had deposited the money in 1994 for a joint business venture with Mr. Driussi, whom he had met in the Grand Cayman Islands.

They decided to open a diving shop in Vancouver and the young man transferred the $23,000 from his home branch in Wiarton, Ont., to a Kelowna branch.

The pair moved to Vancouver and shared a house but the new diving business didn't go well. When the young man went to recover his money, it was gone.

These three stories were reported in the local news and not the national news, which is appropriate because they belong to a local place. When I heard them, I was put in mind of places that I know: sections of Oak Street and Granville Street, Beaver Lake in Stanley Park, this coastal place in which dreams of running a diving business (hatched during vacations in the South Seas) are fully understandable and probably not uncommon. I was drawn to these stories because they are part of a reality that I know, and they lend an aura, a texture, to my imagination of this city and this place.

At the same time, these stories can hardly be said to be stories at all. It is a paradox of the news business that reporters, whom we know to be "looking" for stories, and "getting the story," are permitted (by the convention of objectivity) only to publish the bits of a story that might be called "the facts": dates, names, addresses, ages, numbers of any kind, quoted remarks, etc. These facts are then presented as more or less free-standing, connected to each other only by the silence of the paragraph break.

News stories are accounts of the world stripped of the processes of causality and consequence. Time stands still in news stories, which let nothing flow, and therefore the news can offer no narrative coherence. The news story slices through the narrative, making a cross-section; in this way it is like a photograph, which cuts across time: both the photograph and the story pretend to offer an unobstructed view of the real, but the effect of both of these forms of reporting is to obscure the world even as they seem to reveal it.

But as the "purpose" of the photograph is often confounded by its details (a hand protruding into the margin, a lamppost growing out of a head) so can the "neutrality" of the news story be betrayed by its facts, which, when layered arbitrarily on top of each other, can generate narrative moments that command our whole attention: a second "alleged person" in the drugstore, for example; or two suspects who become a single suspect; stolen licence plates on an unstolen car; something in the black Jetta which repulses the gunman even in his moment of desperation; and what happened to the baby? How is it that children's remains are to be found in a police museum? What was that about a burial at sea? Such moments abound in these accounts, and we can feel narrative pressures building up in them.

These stories are given first as news reports, which must deny the stories that want to be told through them, because stories lead us away from facts and turn us toward the unaccountable. In these three "stories," precisely in what we might call the accident of their facts, looms the enigma of the real, which is never to be measured or explained. (A good story always demonstrates the world; it can never explain it.)

Stories have become rare in cities (and perhaps in the countryside), partly because they are so rare in the news, which is a public space littered with facts and papered over with the lives of celebrities. Stories were already disappearing from the world in 1936, when Walter Benjamin wrote that storytelling had begun rapidly "to recede into the archaic," and was being replaced by "information," a form of communication peculiar to the modern age, whose instrument, he said, was the press—or, as we might put it today, the media.

Benjamin writes that storytellers combine the lore of faraway places with the lore of the local and the past; stories of a place inform first the lives of its denizens, and then the lives of those at a distance who hear the stories from the mouths of travellers returning home. Stories are told and remembered and then told again.

When we pause to contemplate the gunman with the baby at 22nd and Granville, or the hysterical woman with blood on her shoes with the nervous man in Stanley Park in 1947, we are returned to the life of a city, however fragmented, however ridiculous or melodramatic. Even the year 1947 is given back to us as inauspicious and possibly sinister.

These stories recommend themselves to memory, and we claim them for our friends by retelling them. They belong here, to a place to which Jesse James and the czar of Russia have no claim, but to which a man known only as Mr. Driussi of Kelowna will always have a claim, even as he languishes in banishment, a solitary figure thrust into exile by a story and a word.

BULL'S-EYE
OF THE
DOMINION

On the way into the city the driver began to discourse upon the theme of the undeserving poor and I heard myself say aloud: Listen, pal, this is one conversation we're not going to have. I sat in the back seat, perspiring lightly behind the improvised barrier of steel and plexiglass. The driver was young and not easily abashed; within minutes he was analyzing weather patterns and describing a recent drought. I turned my attention to the flat city of my known ancestors and the prospect of other, more vital discourse that awaits one in strange places, at least in one's mind. For this was Winnipeg, once the Bull's-Eye of the Dominion, and I was eager to know it.

I am installed in the heart of the city, in an aging hotel named for a deceased British duke, which appears to have slipped from a threshold of elegance in recent decades: the corners of the paper-veneered furniture are protected by ugly pieces of angle iron; in the washroom there are plenty of towels, but their pile is worn down to knobby grains. The ends of the toilet paper have been folded into vees like the napkins in the silent restaurant downstairs. A hint of historicity offers itself in two framed but unglazed prints: above the console harbouring an ancient television set hangs the image of a man on horseback; he wears a red jacket. The inscription is without sentiment: 1855: General Officer Cavalry. Above the bed another man in a red jacket, this one on foot, holds a sword: 1756: Officer, 24th Foot.

I switch on the television to watch The National grind through its diurnal course. The local news is presented by a woman I knew in college nineteen years ago, two thousand miles from here. I lean forward while she intones in the manner of the trained news anchor, placing the emphasis on all the unimportant words. Her features are more exaggerated than I remember them to be: rouge and lipstick, age perhaps, the camera's intimate scrutiny, make her nose somehow even nosier, her cheeks cheekier and her lips much lippier than they ever were in real life. Heavy metal shards hang from her earlobes. Her red hair is a lacquered shroud, devoid of hairiness. She looks directly at the camera, into my eyes.

I have work to do here in the day, but in the evenings I talk over old times with a colleague and we stroll through the corridors of this most empirical of cities, littered still with the stony accoutre-ments of empire. Something hesitates here: History, perhaps, or Progress—that inexorability that seems always to be moving through our lives wiping out memory. This city, more than others in the west, seems at least to propose memory, if not to preserve it. Too much of the old brick and stone remains, the engraved facades of another age, as if someone had forgotten to tear them down. The glass and steel, the parking lots, are only beginning to take their death grip; shiny towers overshadow but do not obliterate the ornate facades of triangular office buildings, two sides creamy white, the third a dreary expanse of grey brick. These drab third walls imply abrupt removal, the extraction of neighbouring struc-tures. The old city is like an open mouth with half its teeth gone. We wander through streets lined with ancient brick warehouses now undergoing gentrification, and feel the heavy shadow of absent Industry keeping the late sun off the sidewalk.

I look at these heavy remnants of another time, and feel my grandparents' eyes upon them. We pass a low building crowned by an intricate mosaic of small tiles. We are told that once it harboured the YMCA, and I look for my father on his bicycle, coming in from St. Vital. Summers he worked at Eaton's, in the bargain basement, and one year he and his brother modelled underwear for the mail order catalogue: my mother, who came from a better part of town, once showed me the dried out pages bearing the sepia images of young men in long johns. My grandfather was the complaints clerk at Eaton's and worked there long enough to earn the gold pocket watch which he gave to me and which I carried through university and beyond before leaving it behind, somewhere in the past.

People in the street have broad Slavic faces, and the high cheekbones of Cree and Métis. Surely this is another country. We look up into a vast blue dome of sky and see the moon, a pale crescent tattooed faintly into the taut, overarching air. It is the old moon hanging in an old sky, and it seems the very emblem of memory and time. Under that sickle moon forty-five years ago my father pedals home in the late evening through the rumble of the railyards along Main and over the Red River where it joins the Assiniboine. He turns left, but this evening we cross the Assiniboine and turn right into an avenue lined with elm trees, where teenaged girls slouch along the sidewalk and fall silent as we near them, turning their eyes away from ours. We pause in front of a grim cathedral in order to feel it looming over us for a few minutes before walking on to the corner, where we stop at a cross-street that bears my name: Osborne Street. Overhead a green sign proclaims Osborne Village and another points to Osborne Bridge. We enter the village along Osborne Street, and my name is on every corner, on shop windows, outlined in neon above the café. The whole neighbourhood shouts Osborne, Osborne, and I am overcome by a sense of spurious eponymity: an impostor come to claim false inheritance; now it is I who cannot meet the eyes of passersby. Across Osborne Street an open bookstore offers refuge. We cross over to it and I ask the clerk for a book I've been trying to locate for some weeks, and here in Osborne Village they have a copy, which I tuck gratefully into my shoulder bag as we head back along the street toward the bridge that bears my name. Halfway across the bridge we find a bronze plaque fastened to the railing at knee level, oxidized to a dirty green and soiled by exhaust fumes. We crouch down to read a meagre note memorializing another Osborne, a military man whose first name was William, born 1837, died the year before my grandfather's birth, 1887, remembered rather splendidly now for this minor river crossing; but forced in his commemoration to share his plaque with an entire city council, whose names are appended in neat alphabetical rows beneath his own.

So who is William Osborne? One of the Kentucky Osbornes perhaps, as my grandfather's grandfather was? I remember my grandfather saying that his father had fought in the Apache Wars and been wounded in the shoulder, but in the same memory I recall the bullet that wounded my great-grandfather to have been made of silver, so it may be that I am confusing him, or his Apache assailant, with the Lone Ranger, who cast his own bullets in a secret silver mine somewhere in the mythical American West.

Osborne Street widens after the bridge into a broad avenue skirting the lawn in front of a legislative building that might have been plucked whole from a scene in a movie about the British Raj. At ten o'clock it's still broad daylight. We pause near the cenotaph before a cluster of statues: three bronze women in uniform. Looking closely we see Pegasus on the buttons on one of the uniforms, an anchor on the buttons of the second, and the head of Mars on the buttons of the third. The women stand higher than us on a concrete block; the hems of their bronze skirts are at our waists. Beneath the skirts their slim, vulnerable legs, implicitly stockinged in the greenish patina of old bronze, seem weirdly provocative, and I wish to caress them, but don't.

At Portage and Main, once the true centre of a nation, in front of the old Bank of Montreal building, there is another statue, this one a private soldier in full World War I garb: the tin hat, the heavy greatcoat, the boots. He carries a pack and holds a rifle across his chest. He is enormous and solid. There is nothing at all vulnerable about him. That is my grandfather, I say, who refused to tell me stories about that war.

At six o'clock on the last night it began to rain: fat drops widely spaced falling from a blue sky. By seven there were thunderheads over the house to which we had been invited for dinner, and the street was growing dark when the storm broke overhead in a rush of water and thunder, and then the forked lightning. We sat in the enclosed front porch and watched through screened windows as the light changed from yellow to green and brown, then back to yellow again as the wind rose and began to blow the rain horizontally along the avenue. The elm trees threw their long arms into it and thunder exploded over the house, sending forks down into the city. Across the street, shadowy people opened their front doors in order to look out into the storm; I kept close to the window and felt on my face the spray of rain forced in through the screen. Later, from the back of the house, we looked straight out over the alley toward the source of the storm and the sun. There was white light off to one side, and a green cast to the light in the alleyway where the clay track had turned slick and muddy.

The storm passed over and through the neighbourhood, leaving it washed and sparkling wet and glowing in a refulgent golden light. *Refulgent*, I said to myself, now I can use that word. The mesh of the screen gave the scene a gauzy surface, like a pointilist painting. Sirens wailed nearby and far away and we sat out the night in ancient overstuffed chairs that reminded me of my grandfather's burgundy sweater, drinking and talking, enclosed in the surcharged afterglow of a prairie storm.

At noon the next day I walked alone down the shady side of Portage Avenue, leaning away from the prickly heat and the white cloudless sky, and, in the cool basement of the Hudson's Bay Company, bought a hotdog (jumbo, sweet relish and sugared mustard) at the malt stand. Back at the hotel I exchanged a loonie for my luggage and called a cab. I'm going to the airport, I told the driver, but I want to go by the Louis Riel monument and Vimy Ridge Park. That was all right with the driver, although he had to call in to find out where Vimy Ridge Park was. All the windows in the cab were open and the breeze took the sweat from my forehead as we rolled through a maze of side streets and neighbourhoods looking for Vimy Ridge Park. It should be right up there, said the driver, and the sickly aroma of dampened woodfire swept over us as he said: sure enough, it must have been hit. A few teeter-totters and swings, a small stretch of green, and one big tree split in half by the lightning of last night, black and still steaming in the noon sun. Farther along, the Louis Riel monument remained intact, a mysterious huge stone image of a bodybuilder pressing his hands together, reminiscent of the old comic book pictures of Charles Atlas. Well, there you go, said the driver. When you're out at the airport, look for the statue of Billy Bishop, they've got one out there, did you know that? Then he took me to the airport where I made a quick search for a statue of Billy Bishop, but something like fate kept me from finding it.

THE ANARCHIST PERIL

THE LIFE OF THE MIND

Absurd was an absurd name for a principle we either live by or go mad refuting. When I first read Sartre, sometime in my teens, existentialism mattered: I knew what the guy was talking about. There was no depth, no wisdom, in this understanding; it was a purely intuitive reaction to the dour Scottish Calvinism with which I'd been sprinkled at birth, and it used very similar metaphors. It rolled a very appealing reverse on Tennysonian earnestine: Life is real, life is earnest, and—guess what?—its end *is* the grave. While O sea broke, broke, broke on its cold grey stones within sight of my bedroom window, I read *Being and Nothingness* and cried for joy. Everything I'd been perceiving and denying made at last an acceptable species of sense. When I saw the first *Mondo Cane*, in the same period, I seized immediately upon the cargo cult sequence: yes, this was a phenomenon truly *ex nihilo* (the Creation thought impossible even for God)—emerged out of nowhere, though obviously Nowhere existed and meant something, yet believable: there was, in those island tribespeople, a condition of mind prepared for the fallen plane, ready to worship it. They knew what to do with it.

—from "A Literary Education," an unfinished
essay by D.M. Fraser

I

In my teenage years I read Zane Grey while D.M. Fraser was reading Sartre; when he was sneaking in to see *Mondo Cane* I was lining up for *The Abominable Snowman*. This was part of the difference between us. When I knew him it always seemed to me that the Life of the Mind had been open to Fraser all his life, whereas I had stumbled into it at a late age. Fraser proposed that we each write an account of our literary education, which would be separate stories of how we came to be who we were. I was probably drunk, because I promised enthusiastically to do it, and eventually sat down at my typewriter (a magnificent tiny machine called a Hermes Baby) to contemplate a literary education that began with Dick and Jane and not with the King James Bible. This was during a time when I felt myself to have escaped the past, or perhaps to have lost it, with the result that I was unable to write a single word about the life that lay "behind" me. Some years later, Fraser died and I found in his archives fragments of an essay called "A Literary Education," and sometime after that I sat down, this time at a computer terminal, and tried again to contemplate the past.

In grade one, yes, it was Dick and Jane, a dreary text that I read aloud to brother Tom and sister Judy in Edmonton, Alberta. That was Inglewood School, with the frightening teeter-totter in the yard. I bounced down hard at my end and frightened Pam, a blonde girl who shrieked as she flew into the air, and I fell in love with her. The teacher was Miss Nye, a dreamy beautiful woman who drew an enormous *X* over the page in my scribbler and held it up for the rest of the class to see as an example of something no one should do, ever, in their scribbler. Her gesture stands in my memory like a wall, blocking any trace of the ensuing months. My mother wept when she saw my report card because she thought that *H* stood for Horrible—and I resolved in that instant to spare her any further knowledge of my school life.

In grade two Mrs. Martin, a stern motherly figure with red hair, took us through the alphabet one day and one letter at a time, right after morning recess. The alphabet occupied the length of the side wall above the dusty, tantalizing blackboard; I was familiar with all of the letters shown there, and presumed that once we had finished with them we would get to the real, Adult letters after Z. On the twenty-seventh day I pulled out my alphabet scribbler, and Mrs. Martin went on without pausing to some other subject, leaving me blushing and too embarrassed to ask the question.

Grade three was a dark time: it began in a windowless room that was much too large, and the teacher was a man, a mysterious bespectacled person who sat at his desk at the back of the room forever spying on us. We studied the Belgian Congo endlessly, gluing magazine photographs into our Belgian Congo scrapbooks with sticky bottles of mucilage that always made hard spots on the page, and drawing outlines of Africa with the heavy 4B pencil we were not allowed to lose or to sharpen needlessly. Even now that the Belgian Congo is Zaire, I need only to see the name and I can smell the sickly aroma of mucilage and pencil lead, and feel the grotty rough paper in the Belgian Congo scrapbooks.

Our parents took us away from Edmonton in January and I was hugely relieved that my life would not be going on forever in that bleak grade three room, lost in Africa. Where was Pam by now?—gone, already in the past. We went on the train to Kamloops through mountains and endless night. I lay awake beside Tom in the upper berth as long as I could, listening to the train swaying around me and the grandfatherly voice of the conductor who appeared to need no sleep in his great wisdom. When I slept I dreamt for the last time of Kamloops—a place, our parents had said, of many hills. In my dream the hills were small and covered in short grass like the golf course along the Saskatchewan River—each one ringed at its base by small white boulders; there were ponds between them, also ringed with white boulders, and in the ponds, many silver fish; in the Kamloops of my dream the sun shone on the green grass and one wandered among tiny manicured hills, admiring the fish in the ponds. The train stopped in the dark and strangers put us into their car and drove us through a terrifying landscape of dirty snow and evil black ground: such then was to be Kamloops in real life, a grimy inhospitable hillside; and I shrank into myself and locked away my expectation in the back seat of a stranger's muddy automobile.

In Kamloops the blackboards were green, not black, and the teacher was Miss, not Mrs., Martin. Miss Martin installed me at the back of the room behind a girl named Molly. Molly had long brown hair that hung down past the edge of my desk and I wanted to touch it but never did. The green blackboard was a mystery; it seemed to suck into itself everything that Miss Martin wrote on it. At recess I went up to the board and made a line in chalk in one corner, pressing hard. Back at my seat I could see my line as plain as day, and concluded that the problem lay not with the green blackboard but with Miss Martin, who couldn't—or wouldn't—press hard enough. We had to line up one class at a time for the nurse's examination, and when the nurse stood me in front of the eye chart I could make out only the top two rows, one eye at a time. She took me by the hand and marched me out of the room and up along the lineup to the principal's office. I was thrilled to know that there was Something Wrong With Me, but dismayed to hear the nurse telling my mother about it on the telephone. A few days later I returned to the classroom with spectacles on my nose and took my seat behind Molly. Miss Martin made a speech welcoming me back, and then she moved me up to the front row. I wanted to say, I can see now, I'm okay, but couldn't say anything, and so sat out the rest of the year in the front row with my ears burning, hating Miss Martin, the nurse, the Principal—for taking Molly away from me and humiliating my mother.

In the Kamloops public library I started out with Thornton Burgess books about muskrats and beavers and read them all dutifully. But when I found the Hardy Boys, reading became a vice rather than a pastime, and so it has remained ever since. I kept the family flashlight under the bed; when Grant Smith told me that there were some new Hardy Boys in the library I ran all the way down First Avenue and got all five of them and read them in three nights. In grade four we were forced to memorize times tables, and I discovered a way to cheat by using the numbers and the marks on my ruler as if they were fingers and toes. The ruler sat on the top edge of the desk: by staring at it I got all the answers to all the math tests; in September I was whipped out of the grade five room into a desk in the grade six room, surrounded by a bunch of snobby kids older than me by a factor of ten percent of my whole life, as I determined a few days later on my new ruler.

The grade six teacher was a knuckle-rapper. You stood up in front of the class and put out your hand and she smashed her ruler (a heavier, Adult model) onto your knuckles. She was a fierce bony woman as old as time. In her class I learned to daydream; a map of the world hung open on the side wall and every morning I looked at the map and picked out a new sector to put into the daydream. First I had to steal the necessary canned goods and macaroni out of my mother's pantry, then get from Kamloops to Vancouver on my bicycle, and once in Vancouver convert the bicycle into a pedal-raft, cross the Pacific Ocean, skirt the islands of Japan, pedalling ever onward, touching all the pink areas and the green ones, never leaving the hallucinatory flat blue ocean through which I pedalled all that year, avoiding Africa. Only once was I apprehended and called up to the front of the class and whipped on the back of my hands, four strokes each, with the teacher's personal ruler. I became aware, at the moment of her first whack, of my responsibility to her, which was to appear to be admonished, and my responsibility to my classmates, which was to appear to be unvanquished. Everything in life was a dissembling. I ceased after that day to think of my colleagues as snobs, and learned to conceal my daydreaming well enough that it has rarely been detected since.

During this time I began to find real friends, boys whose parents my parents could not know; these boys were my secret friends, and I had only slightly to reinvent myself to become one among them, fiercely driving marbles into the dirt circle; the names I remember are Kane Scott, Wayne Callaghan and Gerry Lacusta. Gerry delivered *The Advertiser* into Chinatown, the scariest part of Kamloops, and I went with him; then when he went away I delivered the paper myself along that mysterious avenue. In grade seven I went to another school and no one knew that I was younger than them. Pearl White and her best friend Wanda sat in the front row and had breasts. Pearl's twin brother Percy was the breast expert among the boys. Percy claimed actually to have seen his sister's breasts, and later in the year to have felt up Wanda after school in the gym. It's a kind of milky feeling, that's what tits are like, he said, and I thought he might be lying because he was confusing flesh and milk. But it was Donny Grafton, whose father was a doctor, who told Tom and me what the word *fuck* meant. You put your dink in a girl's dink, is what he said. Tom and I beat him up and called him a crazy dink asshole but Donny wouldn't relent: he said a ditch digger had told him and that made it seem like it might be true.

The grade seven teacher was grey-haired and plump and fierce-looking, but she never whipped anyone. She gave us an hour a day to read *Kidnapped* silently like adults while we sat at our desks. I read fast enough to read it twice and it was the only schoolbook that I would ever read with pleasure. At the end of the year the teacher took me aside and told me I had a very high IQ. I didn't know what an IQ was, but I knew she was telling me a secret and I kept it a secret for twenty years because I didn't want to lose my friends.

In grade nine in North Vancouver, Neil Todd and I were standing in the back of Mr. Robinson's room after school. Mr. Robinson was the Social Studies teacher. He pulled a piece of lumpy white cloth out of his desk and threw it across the room. Here, catch, he said. He was laughing. Neil caught it and held it up. It was a brassiere. Neil dropped it on the floor. The grade ten teacher was Chinese, a small delicate man named Mr. Locke. Mr. Locke played the piano at assembly, and arranged for parents to take their kids to *Romeo and Juliet* when the Royal Vic came to town. *Romeo and Juliet* was a girl's story and I had no interest in seeing it, but my father bought the tickets and took me anyway. When the curtain rose there was dust glittering in the air of the street and I wanted to know how they did that; but within minutes I had forgotten the dust and was aware only of the story unfolding before me. When it was over my belly was in a knot and I had to hold back my tears because fifteen-year-old boys do not weep in public. I was astonished in the full sense of that word: thunder-struck. Where had all that come from? The grade eleven teacher had a wart beside his nose that he was forever rubbing with his forefinger. He made us read the whole of *Julius Caesar* out loud, as if we were children learning to read, and I developed such a strong aversion to that play that I couldn't get through it ten years later when I set out to read all of Shakespeare.

There is only one teacher of my school days whom I wish to remember and to name—but his name has been lost to me for years. He had a sullen demeanour and thick eyebrows. On the first day of class he sat on the edge of his desk and glowered at us and said, I want you to listen to this. Then he began to recite Chaucer's "Prologue" in a deep baritone that filled the room: "Whan that Aprill, with his shoures soote / The droghte of March hath perced to the roote"—I heard these mysterious words and the hair stood up on the back of my neck. More strange syllables poured from his lips and he went on and on, making a sound and a rhythm that I knew but could not comprehend; he seemed to be speaking the very memory of language. I held onto it as well as I could, tanta-lized and filled with desire, understanding nothing. When he stopped, he said: That is what Mr. Chaucer wrote and that is how he spoke it—when you open your textbooks you will find some-thing altogether different.

Once I had thought that the alphabet would go on past Z, and

I was proved wrong; but my error was merely directional: the truth is that the alphabet starts before *A*.

II

> I have never been to Oxford or London, never made the Grand Tour, never actually seen any of the places in which the nineteenth-century British-European sensibility, if ever there was such a thing, was supposedly formed. I don't much regret these lacunae in my travels. I cherish instead a borrowed book, a superior sort of guide for present-day tourists, which lists comprehensively the Great Historic Places of Europe, country by country, city by city; many of them further represented by handsome photographs. Nothing is said to explain just why the places are great and historic. The implication is that we already know all that, or ought to. It may be unnecessary to go anywhere now: everywhere comes to us, resides in us. I have never walked in Flanders Fields, though after years of schooling I can recite the poem verbatim. I know exactly what I'd see if I went there: poppies, blowing between crosses, row on row. *Pace* Emily Dickinson, who for her part never saw moor nor sea.
>
> —*from "A Literary Education," by D.M. Fraser*

When I was nineteen, in 1966, the springs of literature lay unequivocally elsewhere, in other times and places, most of which were European, or, more specifically, British. There was no shame or irony in this; it was merely the way the world was. When I went to Europe in the fall, Hemingway's books went with me, and—certainly in the south of France, the north of Italy, in Spain and Switzerland—the simple declarative sentence served admirably as a kind of cultural sunglasses for a teenaged boy in foreign lands. What I saw in those countries, and much of what I thought, can be known again today merely by turning to Hemingway; it was that close a fit.

I began travelling with two friends, Peter and Humphrey. We drove the secondary highways in a secondhand English van and sustained ourselves on local pâté and small loaves of bread and cheap red wine. We lingered in cafés and bars, some clean and well-lighted, and watched older men with moustaches maintain their dignity while drunk. In England, where our journey began, I had equipped myself with Fitzgerald's *Tender is the Night*, so that when from a distance we observed the rich in Monte Carlo and Nice, I knew exactly what we were looking at.

I had not been as well prepared for the north of France, perhaps because I had read so little with which to imagine it. We landed at Dunkirk in a cold rain at night, in the fog, amid bleating foghorns and harsh spotlights; the ship that carried us over the channel had been a troop transport in the war; in the noisy confusion of the landing, we felt lost and perhaps mistaken in our plan. We lost our way for a time in a maze of narrow streets; on finding a highway we drove steadily through the night, successfully escaping Dunkirk, only to find ourselves in daylight in a land where war seemed still to be underway. The towns were shuttered up and turned in upon themselves, their grey stone walls chipped and pocked, we supposed, by bullets fired in the first world war, perhaps by our grandfathers. It was the thoroughly black and white memory of photographs of that war that we laid as a screen over the dull brown landscape and its morose inhabitants who seemed never to smile: indeed, when we spoke to them, they responded angrily and turned away: had we misspoken our-selves—or was there something to be ashamed of here? Our goal was Berlin and the Wall: the signal end of the western world. We passed as quickly as we could over the border into Germany.

In the Black Forest we saw our first fairy castles, perched on the sides of distant mountains in precise replica of the castles in our childhood picture books. This was eminently satisfying: narrow pointing turrets and gingerbread battlements. And I remember wandering through an utterly familiar medieval town with its upper storeys built out over the street. The ancient university buildings in Heidelberg were equally familiar, as were the tiny electric streetcars that rattled casually throughout the city. We contrived to remain a few days in Heidelberg by moving the van to a new spot each night in order to avoid the police, whose obsession, we soon learned, was to harass transients mercilessly, and whose uniform—the pushed-up cap, the heavy coat, the high boots—bore a distressing resemblance to the Nazi attire pictured in our boyhood comic books. We were drawn to the bars by the students who frequented them—in particular by a coterie of anglophiles who met nightly in a downstairs skeller and pretended to be English in the manner of Bertie Wooster and his friends in the Jeeves novels: pipe-smoking young men a few years older than us, in tweed jackets with leather elbow patches, who spoke English in the improbable, impeccable accents of a bygone, fictional English gentry.

The highway to Berlin took us through Nuremberg late one afternoon, and we drove unerringly through the city to the deserted and decrepit concrete stadium where we rolled slowly around the field in the last light of day, hallucinating Hitler and the terrifying light shows of the newsreels. A magnificent castle in the city turned out to be a youth hostel; the concierge was a small angry man who took our passports and conveyed us through a dark passageway into a large room at the rear filled with rows of bunk beds. At eight o'clock the doors were locked for the night, at nine the lights went out. One of our fellow inmates pried open a window with bars behind it and we huddled there, smoking *verboten* cigarettes and cursing the place. Later as we lay in bed, the door burst open and the little man came in with a flashlight which he shone in each of our faces as he demanded to see our receipts. We

were evacuated early in the morning, in the dark; it was cold and
raining heavily as we got the van going and swung wordlessly out
onto the highway. For two or three hours we proceeded in silence
and the rain turned to sleet and then to snow. Finally Humphrey,
who was driving, said, This is bullshit—a simple declarative sen-
tence—and we stopped to make coffee and warm ourselves around
the primus. We got out the big map and unfolded it so that we
could see the bottom of the continent, and there, at the farthest end
of highway, lay Greece, a mere U-turn away. The heaviness that
lay among us disappeared as we made the U-turn and began the
downhill run, south, the fuck, as we said again and again, laughing
with relief, the fuck out of this place.

The map of Europe was more familiar to us than any map of
North America; our years of schooling lent a weird resonance to
the topographical features we had confused endlessly in the bore-
dom of the classroom: Pennines, Appenines, Pyrenees; the Seine,
the Rhone, the Rhine, the Ruhr, Rouen, Biscay, Bordeaux, Bou-
logne, Bologna. We all remembered the elusive Firth of Forth
from grade eight, which always turned out to be the River Clyde,
unless you had it the other way around to start with. When we
crossed the Rhine into Switzerland, we knew it to be significant in
a ridiculous way, because we were going in the wrong direction,
and said to ourselves, Retreat Over the Rhine, as if it were a chapter
title (which no doubt somewhere it is). We were going south,
toward Hemingway country, and I began to anticipate another
kind of encounter with imagined places. We drove through Basel,
a city too well-scrubbed to invite lingering, and into the tidy
countryside, where soon we were glimpsing scenes from the foot-
hills sequences in *Heidi*, but now I was reading *A Farewell to Arms*
and preparing myself for quite another country; I found Locarno
on the map and the drably named Lake Maggiore, left nameless in
the novel, and traced the route by which Hemingway allowed
Frederic Henry and Catherine Barkley to escape the war in the
rowboat, from Stresa at the Italian end up the lake in the storm, at

night, to Brissago at the Swiss end, and then Locarno and later Montreux on Lake Geneva. We stopped at Neuchâtel, where a friend was going to school; I wished eagerly to go to Locarno, so that I might observe the landscape of fiction, but Locarno lay on the other side of the Alps, and was approachable only through snow. Neuchâtel, however, had a large lake of its own upon which I was able to transfer the image of the escape from the war, even though it did not lie across an international frontier. We dined with our friend and her teachers, an elderly couple who allowed only French to be spoken at meals. The old man had white hair and a moustache and wore plus-fours; after dinner he poured each of us a thimbleful of his own peach brandy, which we sipped decorously while conversing in broken French. He put me in mind of the retired professor in Hemingway's story "Homage to Switzerland," and I half expected him to produce a membersip card in the National Geographic Society. A heavy snow began to fall and we started the long fishtailing run down into France. As we drove along the shore of Lake Geneva, I imagined Montreux not very far to the east of us, where Frederic Henry would lose Catherine Barkley forever.

In France it was warm and I had *The Sun Also Rises* in the Scribners paperback. Absinthe was nowhere to be found, so we drank Pernod instead. Some days passed before we found a bar (in Marseille, I think) where they left the little saucers on the table to keep track of the bar bill, just as they did in Hemingway's stories; but we never found a waiter who had once gone twelve rounds with the current light-heavy-weight champion. I began to write short self-conscious sentences in my notebook, about Switzerland and the snow, and tried to keep the adjectives out. In Avignon an old woman wearing a beret hailed us in the plaza in front of the cathedral. Vous êtes canadiens? she said, and she began shaking up and down with her hands held low, one in front of the other, imitating a machine-gun. *Ak-ak-ak-ak*, she said, *Ak-ak-ak*, les canadiens. Ils tuent les allemagnes! She was laughing and weeping at the same time. Then she began shaking our hands and patting our shoulders. Just as soon as I could find a café and a certain privacy, I commenced (as Hemingway would say) to put the old woman, with almost no adjectives, directly into the notebook.

Of trout fishing with the dry fly there was no sign, but that might be Spain, which would come later, on the other side of the Pyrenees. Here there was no countryside to speak of; where one town ended another immediately began and, as every night we searched for an empty place to park the van, I felt a hint of the weariness of Europe, where no ground lies unturned, where the dirt has been trod and re-trod by countless generations, where no patch of earth is not soaked in blood. I put that in the notebook too.

We drove in heavy rain through Italy to the city of Florence, which we knew to be the city of the Renaissance, and which we did not know had been underwater for weeks during a great flood. Florence had only emerged from the river Arno the day before we arrived; we were met by the figures of men and women with shovels labouring grimly in open doorways, scooping the contents of their homes into the narrow, twisting streets. We wound our way toward the centre of the city and found the Uffizi palace with its doors open; gangs of workmen were dragging huge paintings draped in tarpaulins into the plaza and leaning them up against the mud- stained walls. We stopped the van and observed this affecting sight for a few minutes and then drove slowly out of the city. Now we would never see the great works so familiar to us from the photographs in our schoolbooks; we had been spared that responsibility by an act of God.

In Venice we were lost for days. There was nothing in Hemingway of this most literary of cities (save a line of ironic dialogue: What news along the rialto? says Doc Fischer in the story about the self-castrator), perhaps because Venice seemed so completely to have been written already. Being lost in Venice was like being lost in a book, in another understanding of time and place, where public and private cross mysteriously into each other and even the outside feels inside, contained in a tangle of alleyways and canals. The museums and galleries were mere extensions of the street and so we went into them easily, to peer through the gloom at Tintorettos and Titians and devices of torture and warfare and the Doge's robes. We felt before these objects an appropriate veneration, and were able by observing them to confirm the photographs that had made them so familiar. We traversed the Bridge of Sighs and the Rialto, we entered coffee bars and restaurants and perambulated the Square of St. Mark, so recently under water. Here was a world of assignation, of private meetings in public places, wholly circumscribed but endlessly mutable. One had merely to look over one's shoulder to see the familiar vanish and then resolve itself into the utterly strange. A few months later I would read *Death in Venice* and, surprised to see precisely the same city in the same way through another's eyes, wonder if there were other places on earth whose purpose would be so clearly to be put into a story.

That day I crossed the Venetian plain: on another day, I promised myself, I too would write such a sentence, resonant with immensity and loneliness. It came whole from the page just as I imagined Hemingway to have written it, and I held it in my mind as we traversed the same plain in the other direction on a grey day in November. I wanted to see the Tagliamento, the river Frederic Henry swims in the novel after escaping the firing squad, but the highway ran instead over many canals and low ditches and I had to content myself with the view of the flat salt marsh, imagining it empty of industry and traffic, save for a passing troop convoy, or the occasional felt glimpse of a man alone in the distance, in flight. We crossed into Yugoslavia and out of the Europe of our schoolbooks, which included no Slavic country, and proceeded down what we had been told more than once was the wrong shore of the Adriatic.

In Yugoslavia we found ourselves with nothing to take our bearings by, save images of the cold war from newspapers and movies—the signal emblem of which was Titograd, a city the colour of iron, whose concrete tenements stepped away in bleak procession over the plateau, in grainy black and white. In Titograd people bundled up against the cold and stood patiently in line to buy groceries. We too took a place in line and pointed at breadsticks, cheese, cans of beans on the shelves behind the counters; no one spoke to us. Everywhere disconsolate young men in grey greatcoats and grey pants and grey caps with red stars on them hung about in little groups, smoking cigarettes and looking over their shoulders. Our first encounter with soldiers had been a few days earlier, in a café in a small town on the coast, where we had passed an evening drinking and singing Christmas carols with a crowd of men in green uniforms. After that we had little communion with the people: in the cities of the interior, stony-faced men crowded up against the van wherever we stopped; we had to press against them to open the door. In cafés we were hissed from behind and occasionally spat at. I tried to put these hostile men into my notebook—unsuccessfully, because I had no way of comprehending them. We passed a night in the mountains and in the morning there was snow on the ground; we opened the door of the van and saw two children standing in the snow, a boy and a girl. We lifted them in and gave them tea and they gave us strings of figs and pomegranates. I had not eaten a pomegranate until that morning. When they got up to leave, we gave them money and they leapt down from the van and ran up the hillside toward the distant silhouette of a man looking down upon us: later we would see a caravan moving slowly across the horizon. In a hotel the clerk grimaced when I leaned over the counter to see where she was putting my passport, and I saw the automatic pistol tucked in under the counter top. It was a very large pistol and it was not in a holster. She thrust the key in my face and looked at me without blinking.

One day we drove to Albania, a country forbidden to foreigners, along a dirt track that dwindled into furrows pressed into the yellow grass. We swung around the end of a big lake and stopped on a hill overlooking a narrow bridge and a little wooden hut. A door in the hut swung open and a man in a greatcoat stepped out. He pointed binoculars at us, and then he began striding up the hill toward us, shaking his head and waving his hands in front of his face.

We got out of the van to wait for the man in the greatcoat, and to look out over the lake, across the valley into the forbidden country, where we could a see another tiny hut and the distant figure of another man standing in front of it, looking back at us. This was a moment in fiction, and we were people in fiction, awaiting an outcome that had already been written.

Just over the border into Greece we picked up a Japanese hitchhiker who bowed to us frequently and spoke no English. A big blue bus thundered by, blasting the opening bars of "Never On Sunday" from its amplified horn. A restaurant proprietor laughed when we discovered how expensive the beer was. She held up a bottle of yellow wine and said, is Greek, is Greek. We bought three bottles and it was very cheap, but none of us could swallow it so we poured the first bottle out onto the highway. We were on the third before we realized that it was meant to taste like turpentine; I remembered my grandfather scraping gum from a spruce tree with his pocketknife and giving me a piece to chew. It was December and warm enough to sleep on the ground at the edge of orange groves. We bought more yellow wine and ate oranges until our gums ached, and we drove by Mount Parnassos with the windows open. Athens lay in a blue haze at the end of a long wide curve of highway choked with weaving trucks and cars and tiny three-wheeled jitneys moving at terrific speed in a din of blasting horns and shouting drivers. We hung on in the middle lane, glimpsing in the distance the apparition of white marble columns suspended above the haze; we saw it again and knew it to be the Parthenon, Temple of Athena, lifted whole from the pages of *National Geographic* and now quite preposterously there, on a low hill in the middle of a vast ramshackle city that seemed, as we fought for position in its chaotic streets, to have been thrown together at the very last minute with whatever materials were lying around.

The world would change for me in Athens, where I took to spending whole days in solitude, prowling aimlessly through narrow streets, rather self-consciously like a character in Hemingway, looking and listening and being there in a way that I had never been anywhere before. In the markets sheep carcasses hung in doorways; strange wailing music hung in the air, and the smell of heavy coffee and frying meat. The streets were crowded with people and everywhere things seemed to be in disarray; shops spilled merchandise onto the sidewalks, and tiny cafés overflowed with tables and chairs. In a side street near the expensive hotels I found a bookstore with a good supply of Penguins; here I discovered Camus and Huxley and Joyce Cary, who were all new to me, and Conrad and Turgenev, whom Hemingway had read, and Dostoevsky and Tolstoy, whose reputations and thick books had until now intimidated me. Every day I walked in a different part of the city, aware of the spectre of the Parthenon lurking in the distance, and sometime in the afternoon I would make my way up to the Acropolis and hang around there until sundown.

In Greece the past lay everywhere in ruins, adjacent to the present yet disconnected from it. I knew nothing of the modern history of Greece, but I had read my father's copy of the Durants' *Life of Greece*, and what little I retained served to intensify the sensation that I felt whenever I stepped onto one of the ancient sites—the barely excavated ruins of Sparta, the fully revealed temple at Epidhavros, or the sections of the Agora that lay exposed in the middle of the downtown market in Athens—that I was stepping through an invisible screen directly into the past. Between the past and the present, temporally speaking, lay only the endless improvisation of daily life—as typified in the makeshift sprawl of modern Athens. Perhaps this is why Athens seemed to fit so well in those weeks: it harmonized with my sense of dislocation. I felt at home in it.

I was not unselfconscious in this, and during the many after-noons I passed on the Acropolis I could never shake a sense of the slight, ridiculous figure I made in such a grand setting. I would stand in one place for an hour, and then move to a new spot and stand or sit there for an hour. I looked out over the city and back into the site and up at the sky. I watched other visitors arrive and depart in small groups and in occasional busloads that pulsed up the hill and broke over the site to pause a moment before surging back down again. I was not the only regular; a half dozen other solitaries were soon familiar to me. We smiled at each other when our paths crossed, but never spoke. The sky was always blue.

At sundown men in blue coats appeared at the bottom of the steps to watch the last visitors leave before locking the gate. One evening as I descended among the scattering of late-leavers, I turned as I usually did to look again at the illustrious ruin and saw the Parthenon precisely as one sees it in a thousand postcard views: ablaze in the low light of a sinking sun. But as quickly as that banal formulation occurred to me, something more happened: the entire assembly of columns, pediments and cornices, the whole prodi-gious structure still ablaze in red light, rose into the air and I could see the sky beneath it before it settled back to the ground. I was filled with a sense of the utterly ridiculous, but at the same time my belly had flipped over and my eyes were filled with tears. I turned around and stumbled through the gate with my head down, away from any who might see, sobbing uncontrollably and gasping for breath.

III

I was nineteen years old in Athens and could feel before me something like the literary life as I had imagined Hemingway to have followed it: in place of the anisette there were small glasses of ouzo that cost 3 cents; instead of tiny raw oysters there was the slice of octopus and a black olive on a toothpick. The youth hostel was a ramshackle walled enclosure not far from the centre of the city; in its shady precincts young people with backpacks gathered from all over Europe, and there were some Australians and even two blond South Africans, who seemed especially lonely, as they were shunned by almost everyone there. The concierge was German, a tiny man in his forties who drank all day and night and cursed bitterly when you banged on the door but never failed to let you in after midnight. There were a few American girls but only one American boy—a penniless draft dodger who seemed fated to a lifetime of aimless drifting. This was the first time I felt the war in Vietnam to be a real thing, and I would have been envious of the draft dodger if he hadn't seemed so debilitated by his exile. As a child I had always assumed that I would eventually be faced with war as my parents and grandparents had been; I carried this unspoken fear with me for another ten years, surprising even myself when, upon turning thirty, the only emotion I felt was relief that now I would never be drafted.

I had been at the hostel a few days when another American appeared, a man from Montana named Roger, who wore a big moustache and maintained a thoughtful air. He was twenty-eight years old, and when I encountered him alone on the stairs I was shy in the face of his great age. In a neighbouring taverna we discovered a shared taste for enormous quantities of cold retsina and fried squid, and I recall this dinner with Roger as the first night of my adult life. What I said I no longer remember, but we had not been sitting very long before we were speaking freely; layers of reticence were stripped away from me as Roger told me about his botched life as a university professor, his divorce, his new girl-friend, his nervous breakdown and his escape from America on a freighter out of New York. In his bag were books by writers still unknown to me, Camus and Kazantzakis among them, and as Roger talked he quoted from them as he tried to make sense of the story he was telling, and I began to understand how books can be used to inquire into life. He spared himself nothing as he talked and I wondered if I would ever be able to speak as openly about myself. He also read his own poetry aloud, reading from a lined yellow pad. They were poems from his life, from the story he was telling, and occasionally as he read them, tears gathered in his eyes. I had never seen a grown man weep, but now I knew it to be possible. This was something that Hemingway had left out.

In the days that followed I continued to prowl the streets alone, lingering in parks and cafés, and usually climbing to the Acropolis at the end of the day. I continued to write short sentences in my notebook and began reading Kazantzakis, who gave me a living Greece, and Camus, who gave me a way to think about myself. Roger lent me his copy of the Fitzgerald translation of the *Odyssey*, and a book of poems by George Seferis. In the evenings I sought Roger out whenever I could, and tried not to appear too solicitous. There seemed to be no difference to Roger between literature and life; he insisted that I locate what I was reading in my own life, as he tried to in his, and I began to see how the life of the imagination can inform life in the world. I preferred to meet with him alone, but I was not the only one who sought him out and frequently there were a half dozen people around the table. These were hilarious, emotional nights and they confirmed me in my decision to stop travelling and to stay in one place. When Roger announced that he had taken an apartment and was going to remain in Greece, I felt justified in my own decision to stay, and wrote a long letter to my girlfriend, who was studying in England, entreating her to join me.

Roger's place was a two-room concrete box set on top of a five-storey apartment block, in the middle of the roof. A spiral iron staircase bolted precariously to one corner of the building was the only way up to the place, which contained a sink and a cold water tap, a hot plate, a cot and a couple of chairs. I went by every few days to make the long climb up the spiral stairs, to look over the machine shops and cheap clothing stores and rundown restaurants of the neighbourhood and to resume a conversation which I hoped would never end.

A week before Christmas my girlfriend arrived on the train, an event that suffused my prospects with new urgency. I had not really believed that she would come; as I sat waiting in the terminal bar (having got there hours before the train was due), I pondered the significance of what was happening. I was elated and not a little frightened. Something irrevocable was certainly in hand: in the morning I had moved out of the hostel and taken a low-ceilinged room near the Plaka with a hot plate, toilet and shower, for eight dollars a week. Somehow I let the concierge know that I was expecting my wife (he knew the French: *ma femme*, I said to him), which I thought to be prudent but knew to be a lie; and as I sat there I considered the subsequent lie that I would have to make, this one by omission, when I next wrote to my parents.

Even so, this was the most literary of moments: I was alone in a foreign country, waiting for my lover (a word so charged that I could not have said it aloud) who was approaching by train from the other end of a continent. Only she and I could know this. As the appointed moment passed and no train arrived, I felt with a shiver the irrational nature of this world in which faith is made to masquerade as reason. And so I reasoned to myself that it was appropriate that the train be late: the aesthetics of the situation could be said even to demand it. I resolved not to inquire but to remain at my table in a limbo from which I might find release only through event and not by will; and the event, when it ensued a few hours later, proved entirely satisfactory. It began with a whistle in the distance and a commotion of porters and officials spreading out on the platform; more whistles sounded and the big diesel swept by in a clangour of screeching metal. Suddenly the platform was filled with people jostling for position. When the train stopped I stepped into the mob and began pushing my way up the length of the platform and back again, caught up in what seemed like an emergency, my eyes burning and my composure evaporating until, by what seemed to be arbitrary chance, I had to stop moving, for there was Sue, standing directly in front of me.

Some weeks later, Sue and Roger and I boarded a decrepit and overcrowded ferry in Piraeus harbour. There were other foreigners on board, some of whom I knew from the hostel, but most of the passengers were Greek families burdened with enormous parcels and live chickens. The donkeys were loaded onto the foredeck by means of a crane and a wide leather strap. It was the last day of the year, cold and blustery, and once out of the harbour the ship began to roll, and seasickness to spread like an epidemic from family to family. There were surprisingly few people on deck, however, so we were easily able to secure space in the open air.

Our first choice had been Crete, which lay more than a day away across the open south end of the Aegean; but a week earlier a ferry returning from Crete had sunk in a storm, taking more than three hundred people with it, among them friends of people we knew in the hostel. So we chose Mykonos instead, a mere twelve hours away along a more protected passage. *Athens lies now behind me*, I wrote in my notebook, trying to match Hemingway ("That day I crossed the Venetian plain"), and knowing as I wrote that I wasn't getting it.

But Athens was by no means behind me. What I had felt at first to be an adventure in that city had modulated, with Sue's presence, into something much more substantial. On my own I had been able to move through its streets leaving no trace; I was, in a palpable way, invisible. But with Sue I was no longer so intangible; for one thing, we learned very quickly that foreign women are never invisible in Greece, at least when they are alone; and I found myself having to break up tangles of badgering men that surrounded her whenever we were parted. There was an etiquette at work in these encounters: it was required of me that I puff out my chest and utter imprecations in English, in this way making my prior claim known to them; they then had merely to slink away. This protocol never failed, but it might be said to have failed us; each of these encounters left us humiliated and distant, without any language that might discharge the humiliation, or—more especially—describe the spurious nature of the prior claim.

The faint trace of my passage through Athens was now overlaid by a more complex imprint informed by Sue's presence; the world seemed to turn toward us, and the events of the world to be mutely bound up in our perceptions of each other. One night in an unremarkable but crowded restaurant, a section of wooden floor a few feet from our table began to lift up. It was a trap door; it remained slightly ajar for a moment, and then it swung open and an elderly man in an impeccable black suit stepped up onto the floor. With one hand he held the trap door open and with the other he assisted an elderly woman, also well-dressed in black, up through the opening. Then he lowered the door, straightened up, looked at us and bowed his head. They looked at no one else, and no one else seemed to be looking at them. They walked silently to the front door and out into the street.

In the Plaka a small man with a toothbrush moustache waved to us from the door of a souvlaki joint; in his gesture there was none of the usual shopkeeper's supplication: he seemed merely to be acknowledging us in the manner of a distant acquaintance. We continued past but then stopped and went back to him. He had a table ready for us just inside the door, a tiny marbletop with wrought-iron legs. As we sat down he placed two shot glasses filled with ouzo on the table and held out an opened pack of oval cigarettes. With another gesture he signalled us to relax while he was busy with his brazier. It felt like we were keeping an appointment and were perhaps a little early. The room was cool and dark and tiny, about twelve by eight feet, with five or six tables. The walls were lined with wicker mats and there were dozens of postcards pinned up at the back of the room, scenic views from all over the world and, right in their midst, a glossy black-and-white portrait of Ernest Hemingway. It was early in the afternoon and the little room was full of people, a handful of older men and another foreign couple somewhat older than us and dressed like beatniks in the movies. They were Americans, very thin and hollow-eyed. The woman looked right through us, but the man spoke up: These are twisted realities, man, he said, very twisted. The proprietor, whose name was Vassilli, busied himself for some time preparing dishes and serving them to his patrons; as he did so he placed dishes in front of us too, although we had said nothing more than thank you. Tiny, delicate souvlakis, roasted tomatoes, more ouzo and coffee and retsina; we nibbled and drank and waited to see why we were there. Eventually the beatniks left and a few of the men left and Vassilli wiped his counter and sat down and introduced himself to us as if he had been waiting all day for just this moment.

In the Athens I remember there are really only two significant places: one is the Acropolis and the other is Vassilli's souvlaki joint. He spoke no English and we had a dozen words of Greek. Yet we sat and "talked" for the rest of the afternoon. Vassilli poured more retsina and the two remaining patrons, older men, joined in the conversation. One of them had enough English to tell us that he was an antique dealer, the other was a capitalist, and Vassilli was a good fellow. At some point Vassilli began cooking again and soon we were eating roast chicken and potatoes and drinking more retsina. Sue and I were getting drunk and were not at all certain what was happening, when Vassilli leaned over and whispered something in my ear and made a warning gesture with his hand. I understood that he was telling us to leave now, so we got up as gracefully as we could. I pulled a handful of money from my pocket, and he pushed it back and ushered us gently into the street. We shook hands with him and he made a circular motion in the air, telling us to come back tomorrow.

We went back to Vassilli's the next day, and each day after that—sometimes for a few minutes, other times for a few hours—for the ensuing weeks. None of these meetings was as extravagant as the first, but like the first, they seemed to share in some prior agreement. We took our notebooks with us and books to read when he was busy; we found that we could pay for our meals by slipping coins onto his counter. On Christmas day Vassilli met us in front of the café so that he could take us home with him on the bus, a long journey into the boxy suburbs, to have dinner with his wife and child and aging parents.

Christmas Eve we had spent with Roger, strolling the crowded downtown streets, and had come upon a murmuring knot of people clustered around a vehicle stopped in the street. We edged our way in and saw that it was a tiny pickup truck from which the cabin had been removed. In the driver's seat a young man seemed to be having a seizure: his head was thrown back and his mouth was open and his arms thrashed grotesquely above his head. He seemed to be trying to turn around, and that proved to be true: he had cerebral palsy. We watched in silence as he struggled to throw his torso backward into the bed of the pickup. Then he forced one arm down into a box and drew out a record. Now we could see what he was up to: his arm trembled as he stretched toward a record player in the back of the truck and lowered the record onto the turntable. Whole minutes seemed to pass as he struggled to settle the record in place and to push a button in the side of the box, at which point a loud crackling erupted from the speaker and then the sound of a children's choir filled the air: a chorus of pure, delicate voices that might have belonged to angels. The crowd of onlookers broke into applause; a shower of coins fell into the back of the truck. The young man groaned triumphantly and wrangled himself back into his seat. He knocked his arm against a lever and the truck rolled down the street in a cloud of song.

Sometime after midnight Sue and I found ourselves in Omonia square. A man with a wheeled cart was selling hot drinks from a brass kettle warmed with glowing coals. *Salippa*, he said, is good. It was thick and hot and full of cinnamon and spices.

Mykonos was a tiny world of whitewashed stone and plaster under a painfully blue sky. There were no winter tourists at that time, and we found an apartment overlooking the sea for thirty

dollars a month. There were no automobiles on the island; every-
one walked or rode donkeys. We too walked, up and down the
coast and across the island, peering into the dozens of tiny domed
chapels, greeting farmers on their donkeys and many hunters of
tiny birds, the corpses of which they wore on strings around their
necks like wreaths. Here Sue could walk alone without harass-
ment, while I sat trying to make sentences in a waterfront café. Sue
was not entirely safe: one day our landlady's brother locked the
door of his textile shop behind her and she had to fight him off.
His name was Petrov; he was an older man, very rotund, and we
didn't speak to him after that, although one night in a taverna a
pitcher of retsina appeared on our table and when we turned
around there was Petrov a few tables away with his wife and
family. He was smiling at us graciously.

Mykonos was a village of older people and children; we met
almost no one our own age; they were all gone to the cities for work
or school. A handful of foreigners lived there: a retired English
couple who owned a villa on the hill overlooking the town and
served expensive brandy in cut glass; a Swiss couple about Roger's
age; and a few Americans a little older than him, all of whom
claimed to be writing novels. Roger was the intellectual centre of
our life there. We met in the evenings in one taverna or another,
eating and drinking and talking as long as we could. We visited
the birthplace of Apollo at dawn; this was Delos, an island temple
awash in light and reverence, where by law no person may pass the
night. Here I wrote my first haiku; we ate bread and cheese atop a
sheer cliff adorned with white marble columns and watched the
sea batter the land. We returned at night and heard music issuing
from the door of a butcher shop. Inside two men playing bouzoukis
were following a third man on a goatskin bagpipe. They were old
men with white hair and beards. The air was redolent of raw meat
and the room was full of older men and women on stools, some
singing and others keeping time with their hands. Stools were
found for us so that we too might make a celebration.

The one horse on the island belonged to a man named Koriakos who was unusually tall and wore a cowboy hat and boots and rode in a western saddle. He was known as The Cowboy, and occasionally in the evenings he would ride into the village along the wide avenue facing the sea, looking much like Clint Eastwood in *A Fistful of Dollars*. We were warned by a gentle old man named Yorgos that Koriakos was trouble and so kept our distance from him, although Roger was forced to face him down one night when he and an American woman were dancing in a taverna and Koriakos interposed himself between them. The confrontation resolved itself into a drinking competition accompanied by the eating of hot peppers: Roger was sick in bed for two days afterwards, but the woman was able to slip away, and to leave the island on the next boat.

Eating and drinking held great ceremonial significance on Mykonos; in the tavernas gifts of food and retsina frequently appeared on our table, sometimes anonymously, and we were never sure how to reciprocate. One day a well-dressed man of about thirty introduced himself to us in the street and invited us to his wedding, which was to be held the following day. The procession followed a track along the shore to a tiny chapel, where we stood outside among a crowd of well-wishers and watched through the window as bride and groom, wearing miniature crowns attached by a golden cord, circled the altar hand in hand. Tiny women in black distributed rice to the crowd and we flung it at the newlyweds as they came through the door. The wedding feast took place in the largest taverna on the island, with a five-piece orchestra playing frantically in the corner. Eventually the groom performed a vigorous solo dance that brought the sweat to his brow. When it ended three men in the front of the room, one of whom was Koriakos, pushed their table, which was laden with plates of chicken and vegetables and bread and bottles of beer and retsina, out onto the dance floor. The orchestra began playing and the groom went down on his knees and grasped a corner of the table in his teeth. Then he stood up and repeated his dance with the table hanging from his mouth, and the plates and bottles smashed onto the floor and he crushed them into the mess of food and drink beneath his feet.

I was reading *Crime and Punishment* by then, and the wedding dance seemed a perfect emblem of a world driven by passion and mystery, embodied in the figures of the fiercely dancing groom and the menacing cowboy Koriakos. We had been on Mykonos three months when Koriakos began to appear more frequently in the cafés and tavernas, and to send gifts of food and drink to our table. One night he took the table next to ours and began talking to Sue while looking at me—rather malevolently, I thought. Koriakos spoke no English, but we learned that he had two fishing boats as well as the horse, and he seemed to be offering them to Sue. With his forefinger he traced the outline of a house on the tablecloth and then looked meaningfully into Sue's eyes. Finally he leaned over and put his hands on the table in front of me, and began tracing figures that I couldn't make out. He did it again, slowly, and I saw that he was tracing Greek letters: Lambda, Sigma, Delta, which I finally understood to mean LSD. He was looking at me intently. I looked back as intently as I could and said, in Greek: no thank you, please. I felt distinctly goofy. Koriakos fell silent then, and a few minutes later we got up and left.

By this time we had begun to think of leaving Mykonos: Koriakos remained for us a somewhat threatening figure, and the mail had stopped; a strike in the Athens post office was said to be the cause, and it was expected to last for months. One day we were simply ready to go, and so we did. Roger held us in his arms at the end of the long quay; we boarded the launch and looked back as it swung out to the ship, watching him grow smaller in the distance.

Our long journey from Athens to Spain felt more like flight than travel. The train out of Athens was jammed with passengers and more people kept getting on as we proceeded north toward Yugoslavia. There was a kind of panic in the air; people wore grim expressions and huddled silently in corridors. In Yugoslavia more cars were added to the train and we found a compartment whose lone occupant was a man of about thirty who welcomed us eagerly and stationed himself at the door, where he refused entry to those left standing in the corridor. He was a shoemaker on his way to Germany with a bagful of bread and sausage and wine, all of which he pressed on us; he traced our feet on sheets of paper and we wrote our addresses on them, and we left him in Milan to push our way onto another overloaded train. We learned that striking railworkers were closing down the lines all over Europe; this was the last train to Marseille, and in Marseille we pushed our way onto the last train to Spain. The whole continent seemed to be closing down behind us.

Along the Costa Brava in Spain, menacing policemen carrying sawed-off shotguns trudged up and down in the sand. I reviewed my notes and calculated that I had read a hundred and fifty books since leaving home; I could remember each one of them. In *Time* magazine we read accounts of the coup in Greece, which had turned the country into a police state mere days after we left it. Later we would hear from Roger, who went back to Athens to find tanks in the streets; his favorite taverna had been closed up and its proprietor, a garrulous left-wing Englishman, was nowhere to be found. We heard nothing from Vassilli, and a few years later when I asked friends going to Greece to look for him on Ermou Street, they found no trace of him. Our escape from Greece had been inadvertent, and again I felt the absence of history in my life, which is perhaps not to be regretted.

At the bullring in Alicante we watched a number of bulls put to death unpleasantly; the crowd was not large and many objects were hurled at a young man whose sword flew into the air each time he thrust it into the withers of the bull; in the end he resorted to a dagger with which he severed the spinal column at the neck, and the body of the bull slammed instantly to the ground; it was as if he had turned it off with a switch. I had just read *Death in the*

Afternoon, and I may even have had it with me at the ring, so I was protected from the force of these events by the literary haze with which Hemingway obscured them.

Such then was my literary education. Sue and I went home separately; I landed on a blustery day in Montreal. When I got into the street I saw men wearing galoshes, a thing never seen in Mediterranean lands, and the image of those mud-stained rubber boots with their zippered flaps filled me with sadness: they seemed the very emblem of regret, and loss, and home.

THE ANARCHIST PERIL

When we were publishers in the seventies, we doubled ourselves up in order to increase our numbers without increasing the budget. So Brian Shein was also Jean-Paul Cortane, who was our radical French thinker, and my brother Tom was Big Bill Stevenson, the guy who collected overdue accounts. We had a resident bourgeois critic named George Telford, who was D.M. Fraser in another life, and difficult rejection letters were usually written by V. Heisstderhundt (which I think means "what is the dog's name?" when spoken aloud in the language of Goethe) who was Jon Furberg at most other times. We were a shoestring operation publishing literary books and broadsides and a four- page magazine that sold for three cents a copy. Our offices were a couple of rooms at the top of an old three-storey walk-up across the alley from the Marble Arch beer parlour, which was one of the few real beer parlours left in the city. The Marble Arch was where where we did most of our thinking and talking.

The most cosmopolitan amongst us was Jean-Paul Cortane, who was well read in several languages and would go on to study Arabic in later years. Jean-Paul Cortane was good at writing English sentences like this one: "The possibility of freedom is the nightmare of those who choose to sleep in the chambers of oppression"—which is from the introduction to a pamphlet entitled "The Psychology of the Anarchist," translated by Jean-Paul Cortane from an essay originally published in Paris in 1894. The author of the original essay was Augustin Hamon, a "social scientist" given to frequent use of the expressions *a priori* and *psychic manifestation*. M. Hamon's text is a wonderful example of spurious science, consisting largely of the answers he received from "a certain number of anarchists" to whom he put the question: "how and why did you become an anarchist?" This he claimed to be "a variant of the inductive method, confirmed by deduction"—through which he was able to "construct the psychology of the anarchist." His central finding was that the anarchist type invariably demonstrated "the spirit of revolt," a conclusion he was able to support with many testimonies, including these, from three different anarchists: "Victor Hugo put the spirit of revolt into my heart"; "I went without eating—my spirit of revolt showed itself"; "The bourgeois family setting gave birth to my spirit of revolt."

This was a low-budget publication, printed on newsprint and saddle-stitched, and we sold it for twenty-five cents. It was to be the first in a projected series of little-known texts that Jean-Paul Cortane dubbed The *Anarchist Peril*, and which, in an afterword to the Hamon translation, he characterized (characteristically) with these words: "Liberty, revolution, irony: such is the nature of the peril advanced by our series."

And so *The Anarchist Peril* was released into Canada. We sold the first run and printed another and five years passed. Then one day in May of 1978, a Quebec Tory MP rose in parliament "on a matter of urgency," to reveal to the world that our publishing operation, recipient of a Canada Council grant, was a terrorist organization under investigation by Canadian security services and publishers of a book called *The Anarchist Peril*, which "followed the terrorism of the Italian Red Brigades." Our little pamphlet had become a weapon in someone else's war of words. Here was an irony that even Jean-Paul Cortane had not foreseen. The Red Brigades, a frightening band of middle class knee-cappers, had a week earlier murdered Aldo Moro, a prominent Italian politician. A photograph of Moro's bloody corpse had been on the front page of every newspaper in the world, and repeated on every TV screen; it had become the icon of terror in the world.

The appeal of translation is that it posits a priori an elsewhere; translation is proof in itself that other places exist, and that messages, perhaps even truths (for which we always yearn), may emanate from them. The translation is always exotic, always promising whatever we hope to find there. Over the years we would publish many translations, some of them more substantial than *The Anarchist Peril,* but all of them would share these essential qualities. One of them was *The Minimanual of the Urban Guerrilla,* a forty-pager that went for seventy-five cents, and another was a full-blown book called *Wie Alles Anfing (How It All Began)* that went for two ninety-five. The Minimanual was the work of Carlos Marighella, a Brazilian urban guerrilla who died in the sixties, and Wie Alles Anfing was the memoir of Bommi Baumann, a West German urban guerrilla who had renounced violence and left the terrorist movement. The Minimanual was a straightforward account of guerrilla tactics (not much on strategy) and we lifted our translation straight out of a Black Panther edition that had gone out of print in the U.S.A. The West German book, which had been banned in Germany and carried an introduction by Heinrich Böll, came to us in a rough translation that needed a lot of work before it began to take on in English the direct, somewhat breathless energy that carried it as a narrative in German. Fraser and Furberg and I did this work, along with Norbert Ruebsaat, who was a friend of Jean-Paul Cortane's and a native German speaker. We met at the typesetting machine in the evenings over a period of a few weeks, with plenty of beer, the rough English version, the German version and a French version that had been published in Paris by *editions de minuit.* Norbert would render the German, Furberg the French and Fraser the English. Then we would toss sentences around until they felt right and I would key them directly into type. This collaborative approach to translating was noisy and hectic, but greatly satisfying.

When the book came out it became a bestseller and we realized that we had made a great marketing move (our first) by retaining the German title, *Wie Alles Anfing*, which we printed in big fierce type beside a grainy shot of Baumann in handcuffs.

Such was the perilous work of those days. On a Friday morning in May we began to understand the nature of that peril when a television crew burst into the office and the guy with the microphone said, "is it true that you people are terrorists?" That night the TV news ran an item on Aldo Moro's funeral (complete with emblematic photo of the bloody corpse), and followed it with an opening shot of our little office, which looked, to our dismay, as if it *were* a terrorist's office (whatever that is): there was a grungy headquarters kind of look to the place, enhanced by the little TV logo for terrorism (a fist and a pistol in silhouette) in the upper corner of the screen, and then there were the terrorist publishers themselves, an unsavoury crew of malcontents grimacing uncomfortably before the camera: these guys *looked like perpetrators*; there could be no doubt about it. There were three of them there in that office on the screen, beneath the terrorist logo: George Telford, Big Bill Stevenson and me. (Jean-Paul Cortane had already gone underground.)

Minutes after the TV crew left the office, reporters from the other media began calling and knocking on the door. Their questions all followed the same formula, mixing phrases from one list: "Is it true?" "Do you believe?" "Do you agree?" etc.—and matching them with phrases from another: "Support terrorists"; "Murder of innocent (always innocent!) women and children"; "Knee-capping and assassination"; "Using public money for terrorist purposes"; etc. All of which can only take no for an answer and all of which translate, in reporter-ese, into: "denies that he supports" ("believes," "agrees," etc.). We were perceived to be guilty of "terrorist thoughts" if not terrorist acts, and there was no room for discussion or rebuttal, only denial. This news-mongering process worked in a spiral: within a few days reporters were calling public libraries and harassing librarians who "admitted" having our books on their shelves; in these confrontations the mix-and-match questions began with "did you know" or "are you aware," which were also the questions put to our bank manager and the functionaries of cultural funding agencies—all of whom had to say, of course, that no, they did not know, they were not aware; and they looked foolish in the media, and we looked dangerous in the media. By the following week editorials were appearing in newspapers across the country condemning us for, among other things, breaking Canada's trust with NATO and giving (as the *Windsor Star* put it) "one or two thousand persons the potential to train and wage guerrilla warfare."

Over the next few weeks, and then at longer intervals for the next few years, we were visited by a series of clean young men with short hair, pressed shirts and loosely knotted ties. The most spectacular of them wore reflector sunglasses and shiny white shoes and carried a plaid sports jacket over his shoulder. His story was much like the others: he was in the neighbourhood and thought he'd pick up some of "those political books" he'd been hearing about. We sent him down to the bookstore on the corner, as we did his colleagues, but neither he nor his colleagues ever showed up there. At the same time the telephone began acting strangely, and we took to lowering it out the window when meeting with authors or anyone else we didn't wish to embarrass. The phone had a long cord and it hung down the outside of the building to the second floor where the receiver twisted slowly in the wind at the end of its spiral cord.

But the call from Ottawa came not from the Secret Service; instead it was another Tory MP, in the person of an aide who wanted to know "if it was true" that we had published a set of instructions for setting fire to public buildings. He wanted to send someone around right away to pick up a copy. "This is a direct request from a member of parliament," he said. Then he said, "Look, we can guarantee you terrific publicity on this. It'll be good for you and good for the member. It's all publicity. We'll even fly you to Ottawa." The instructions he desired so ardently were to be found in *The Application of Fire to Public Buildings*, which was my first successful literary effort. It had been inspired by a description (in one of Taylor Caldwell's many terrible novels) of the destruction of New York City by communist-led mobs. In the passage that caught my eye, these mobs are to be seen rampaging through the streets, turning over automobiles and, in Caldwell's words, "applying fire to public buildings." I was captivated by this phrase (I wondered how you would actually do that), and translated the results of my meditation into a broadsheet that sold many thousands of copies.

The media calls had us all on edge; soon no one was willing to answer the phone and George Telford was refusing even to go in the office: we had to go to the beer parlour if we wanted to talk to him. It was clear to us that none of the reporters had read any of our books, nor were they ever likely to; they were feeding off each other instead. Their questions were designed only to keep the process going. We considered our situation at length in the beer parlour and then Norbert said: "You have to turn it back on them. When they ask you a question, you ask them one." The next day I agreed to a phone interview on a local talk show. After a brief introduction, the interviewer began by saying, "Now sir, is it true that"—and when he finished the question I waited a second and said, "You haven't read a single one of our books, have you?" Another moment of silence followed and the line went dead. That was our last contact with the media.

Next day we resumed our work as publishers of *The Anarchist Peril*.

YEVTUSHENKO
IN OKLAHOMA

I wanted to put forever from my mind the day in 1974 when the State Department brought Yevtushenko to town, and that night Yevtushenko went for dinner at Orestes on Broadway along with a hundred or more close friends and admirers. My brother and I and a few friends had made the posters for Yevtushenko's reading at the art gallery earlier that day in exchange for admission to the reading, but functionaries at the door had refused us entry, so my brother and I and our friend D went to Orestes too, in order to collect payment in kind for our labour.

We got to Orestes in time to find a table near the kitchen just as the place was filling up with celebrants. For the next several hours we dined extensively on calamari and olive salad with goat cheese and artichoke hearts in it, and beef morsels on skewers and carafes of retsina and ouzo in little glasses with bits of octopus on the side—while observing dispassionately the antics of the well-dressed crowd, many of whom were academics and government functionaries, very few of whom were as young, as penniless or as cynical as we were. We amused ourselves by making boisterous toasts to Poetry, Lovers of Poetry, Lovers of Russian Poetry, the Bourgeoisie, the Revolution, and of course the State Department, the long cultural arm of which was picking up the tab.

It seemed a point of honour that we remain in Orestes until everyone else had gone, and so we did, never sharing eye contact with the author of *Babi Yar*. The lights went on, the Zorba music ceased, and in the bright precipitate silence that followed, five young men in white jackets gathered in a coterie around our table; one of them held an invoice in his hand. Eventually the one with the invoice said: look, if you just sign here we can all go home. The invoice was for thousands of dollars. I took it and scribbled something on it and gave it back to him and the three of us made our way on foot back to our place on Fourteenth where there was a two-six of two-crown whiskey in the kitchen. We took it outside and got into the back of the '58 Pontiac four-door that my friend R had given me in lieu of the twenty-five dollars he thought he owed me. Later our friend J opened the door and said, that cheap shit makes you ugly, you know, drink the good stuff you won't get so crazy. Then he slammed the door. The three of us were lined up like ducks. Eventually my brother and I had to get out in order to throw up while D, who was implacable in drink, stayed put in the back seat, uttering maledictions against the pruney-lipped functionaries of power and their immaculate spouses.

Much later there were voices in the street and the terrible sound of shattering glass. A dog began to bark and then the geese woke up. I don't remember who the voices belonged to, nor what glass was broken. Already I had begun the long process of putting the night away forever from my mind.

Twenty-one years later, when I heard that Yevtushenko was back in town, I felt a twinge of something like conscience pass over me and then I remembered J warning us about the two-crown before he slammed the door. The twinge had nothing to do with Yevtushenko. Mere hours later, when friends called to invite me to join them for dinner with Yevtushenko, I could think only that much must have happened in the last twenty-one years; for one thing, thank heaven, I was at least that much older now.

It was the weekend of the celebration of VE Day, and the senior downtown restaurants were filled with men in uniforms and women in old-fashioned finery; after some work on the phone we secured an empty table at a more junior establishment. The three of us met in the bar of the Hotel Vancouver where Y was staying, and where a small group of well-wishers had gathered to shake his hand and congratulate him on his new book, the title of which—*Don't Die Before You're Dead*—seems an unfortunate choice to my ear, although for all I know it translates into some kind of near-koan when you put it back into Russian. I drank coffee and sipped soda water. I felt restrained, perhaps even wary. Y drank Calvados and spoke graciously; he was wearing a beautiful Guatemalan jacket and an embroidered cap that seemed to me to embody Slavicity, although I had no way of knowing that it wasn't Guatemalan as well. He was taller than any of us and thinner and he looked like a very long elf. On the way to the restaurant I asked him if he remembered the dinner at Orestes twenty-one years ago and he said, Yes, I will never forget it; I got back to Moscow and there was an invoice in the mail for two thousand five hundred dollars from the restaurant. I even remember what it said on the invoice: Dinner with Russian Poet Yevgeni Yevtushenko and Vancouver Intellectuals. Nothing like that has ever happened to me. Eventually the Canadian Embassy took it away, you know, because of the embarrassment.

When Y told this story I too felt embarrassed, but only as a citizen embarrassed for his country. At that moment I could recall only my brother and me and D at the table in the back of Orestes eating and drinking to excess. I said to Y: I remember that night too, I was there with friends but we weren't part of that, we were trying to be separate from it: we paid our own bill, I'm sure of that. I couldn't say any more because I had no more to say: this was all that my memory afforded me. Then Y said: I went to Ottawa a few days later and there was a party in the hotel, it was a BYOB, you know that expression?—so I brought a case of champagne, and the next day they made a petition to Trudeau to pay the hotel expense. They ask me to sign, but I didn't sign. You understand?

Later that night I told my friend M about Orestes and how my brother and I and D had got drunk in the Pontiac, but we at least had paid our bill, and so for many more days would I remember things to have been that night.

At the restaurant we nibbled on broiled salmon and steamed prawns in spicy sauce and consumed many bottles of a superior local wine. Y maintained himself gracefully in the posture of Visiting Dignitary with Things to Say with Slavic Exuberance; we maintained ourselves equally as Local Dignitaries Not Quite Yet Having Run Out of Questions to Ask in All High Seriousness. Y kept an unlit cigarette in his mouth for most of the evening. It got brown on the outside and rather disgusting. When the waitress appeared at the table Y said, You should know that I am a womanizer. She said, Thank you for letting me know that right away. Later Y recited a couple of poems, leaning over the table toward us like a conspirator.

Out in the street Y described VE Day in Lenin Square in Moscow; he had been ten years old then, an entrepreneur in cigarettes. The square was crammed with people celebrating the end of the terrible war. Many brought record players into the street and the air was filled with the wild scratchy sounds of a thousand melodies. That day he gave away all his cigarettes.

As we walked back to the hotel, Y took me by the arm and said he was tired of all this, going from city to city to talk about his books. It made him tired and he wanted to stop, to stay at home with his wife and family in Oklahoma, so that he could write the books that were still left for him to write.

Many days passed; twice I heard Y on the radio talking about his new book. Soon he would be back in Oklahoma, a place quite outside my imagination. I felt oppressed by something, but what it was I couldn't say. When I sat down to write there was a weight in my mind and I had to sit for a long time before that night at Orestes began to come back; at first I could see only my brother and D; we are angry and drunk and arguing with the waiter, who wants to go home. Then I could see the invoice in my hand: I sign the back of it and add, For the Secretary of State, Ottawa. For a few moments I could see nothing more, but then the memory completed itself, and I could see my hand continuing to write on the back of the invoice, furiously now, forming precisely the words that Y remembered: Dinner with Russian Poet Yevgeni Yevtushenko and Vancouver Intellectuals.

NOSTRUM

The outsider, even the native outsider, is invisible in
Nostrum, which sees only what it sees fit; to be here is,
in effect, not-to-be.

—*from "Prelude and Theme," by D.M. Fraser*

D.M. Fraser was a writer of great talent who died at the age
of thirty-eight in Vancouver, in 1985. He published two collections
of stories during his lifetime and left the world a small archive of
journals and drafts and parts of a novel. He was admired by other
writers for the beauty of his prose and the intensity of his conver-
sation. I worked with him for many years in Vancouver, where he
pursued a literary life in precarious circumstances until his death
from general metabolic collapse, an event that left me stunned and
emptied out by grief; at the wake, which was held at my house, I
was unable to speak in front of the other mourners. Then one day
as I was riding the number 17 bus, I saw the apparition of his face
rise into the sky from behind the mountains in the north; I got off
the bus and the image was still there. It was not Fraser, it was his
likeness, smiling and rather handsome, hovering over the city like
an immense photograph taped to a stick; it was a perfectly bland
sunny afternoon in the city, and I remember that earlier in the day

I had been offended by the unrelenting pleasantness of the weather, which had become a pitiless reminder of the emptiness of all things. Now as I stood on the sidewalk I heard Fraser's voice speak into my ear and then his apparition vanished from the sky. It was an hallucination and a blessing and the beginning of a restoration to the world.

He said that he had come to the west in order to escape from the east, and every year he returned home by day coach on the train to a town in Nova Scotia, the name of which I could never remember, where he remained for a month or two before escaping again to the west, on the day coach. In his fiction he named the place Nostrum, and Nostrum was all that I knew of his home while he was alive. Nostrum was a tiny city on the eastern seaboard, Presbyterian, bleak and coal-mined out: a childhood site, a landscape littered with abandoned mine workings and felt memories; a point of adolescence and departure, leavetaking, egress. Nostrum was his pending work, the heart of it.

In 1987, in September, I went to Nova Scotia for the first time, to attend a meeting of book publishers at an off-season resort near the town of New Glasgow, which was the town that Fraser went home to, the name I could never remember. When the weekend was over I looked up Fraser's mother in the phone book and called her up.

In New Glasgow the red brick high school sits on a hill with its back to the view. An imposing archway frames the main door and smaller arches at the sides are marked BOYS on one side, GIRLS on the other. I imagine Don as a pupil there as I walk up the hill to his mother's house from my room at the Peter Pan, a motel selected for me by the cab driver, who had said that he knew the Peter Pan to be "safe." Don's mother tells me that Don graduated from the high school in Glace Bay in 1964 and he never went to school in New Glasgow. Don's graduation portrait sits on the piano in her front room beside a picture of a kindly-looking square-faced man with a brushcut and a clergyman's collar. That's Don's father, she says; he had been a minister in the Presbyterian Church. Don at eighteen looks a bit like his father but not much; he wears a gown and high collar, and the photographer has him pointing his face off to the side and up in an uncomfortable adolescent pose, a loose assembly of ears, neck and nose. His eyes, though, are eager, even startled, and I feel an implied futurity in the uncertain half-smile, the weird haircut of another time.

At the other end of the piano sits a picture of Don looking up from a typewriter twenty years later in Vancouver. This is the man I knew, bearded and thoughtful, his features composed; and I see now that he grew up to look like his mother, whose face in the kitchen window I had first glimpsed as I came across the lawn. I wasn't sure that I recognized her until she swung open the front door and I saw Don's familiar features in the narrow cheeks, the compact forehead, the neat little hollows behind the eyes. She keeps her chest up and looks directly into my eyes. She may be sixty or seventy years old. Her bones are small and delicate, as were his; her voice rasps like his did, and she too speaks in complete sentences.

Don's mother's house has one floor and a basement, a garage at the side and a lawn in front. She takes me on a quick tour through the place, which she had built twenty-two years ago when her husband died. We go into the kitchen and then to the rear where a tiny foyer leads to a bathroom and two bedrooms: hers is decorated in pink; on the vanity sits a picture of a small boy tucked into the frame of the oval mirror. She plucks it from the mirror and hands it to me. I see a boy in shorts turned round to look at the camera: he's going somewhere; on the back is a pencilled note: Don's first day at school. The other bedroom was for Don when he came home summers and holidays from the university at Wolfville, and then later from out west. Her sister is staying in Don's room, although she's not home right now, and I can see a shelf filled with books against the wall, but we don't go in there. In the kitchen Don's mother makes coffee, puts out homemade doughnuts and an ashtray. This is my first time in Nova Scotia, so we talk about that, and I understand that she will take me to the cemetery, although neither of us mentions it. We stand by the piano for a while, looking at the photographs, until it seems like a good idea to go for a drive.

Don's mother has to sit up straight to see over the dashboard and she retains full command of the vehicle, frequently checking the rearview mirrors, hesitating at intersections and crosswalks. She drives a Ford compact. She has always driven Fords, she says—ever since her husband passed away, which is when she had to learn to drive. We cruise along the dozy main street in Stellarton and then past rows of blocky miners' houses to the Presbyterian Church and the manse they were living in when Don was born. The manse is a handsome building, high, white and gabled. "We froze in that place," Don's mother says. "It was cold as Greenland in there. Don wasn't actually born there of course—we went in to the hospital in New Glasgow for that." I look over at her and then turn my eyes away, surprised by a subtle tug low in my belly, and for a moment I am bewildered by maternity. I want to ask a question I cannot formulate.

In Westville there are more miners' houses, but few mining families live in Westville now. The underground works are shut down and the superstructures have been dismantled. Don's mother says the mines were closed finally because of the explosions, which were frequent and terrible. Now the earth beneath us is a honeycomb of empty shafts and tunnels. Only one mine remains, just outside of Westville, hidden from the highway by high banks of scooped-up earth. Then a stretch of rolling woodland, maple trees turning red among the short spruce and pine and the tangled underbrush. Memorial Gardens is up the hill in a clearing overlooking the river valley. We drive in along a winding gravel road and when we pull up beside the chapel I know that we are going to see the grave. It's windy and cold and there are no other people in sight. Over toward the river the distant sky is bright blue and the hillside on which we stand lies in the shadow of a heavy bank of cumulous cloud which seems to press down upon us.

The Atlantic sky is lower than the Pacific sky and the light is much redder. Don's mother says I really should have a coat at this time of year. She leads the way over the rising ground toward rows of markers lying flat in the grass and then suddenly there it is at my feet: DONALD MURRAY FRASER. 1946–1985. "That's it," says Don's mother. I have never visited a grave before. The plaque lies embedded in a concrete block sunk into the ground. "It's a headstone, you see," says Don's mother. Headstone: I wonder if that means his head is right beneath it. "His father is over here," she says, and when I turn around she is standing behind me next to a second row of headstones. A plaque with Don's father's name on it lies directly in line with Don's and there is an empty space beside it. "This is my place here," she says, pointing at it. "So you see, we'll all be here together." She takes in the three plots with a simple gesture. "Not that it matters much, I suppose," she says. I stand at the side of Don's grave, careful not to step on it. The ground is springy where it's been cut up and reassembled, and there's a kind of valve or cap in the middle of the headstone, an anchor, perhaps. Don's mother has come up beside me. "1946," she says. "He was born in April, you see. He would have been thirty-nine in just a few weeks." These are the things one talks about at graveside. Don's mother steps back to give me a little distance. I've been unsure about my hands ever since we got here. Wondering what to do with them: stop thinking now and look; be still. Feel the swollen ground, stand and look down. Confess the dear bones, the earth. Femur, tibia, clavicle, skull. I would hold them in my hands. I say to myself: wait.

Back in the car Don's mother says she comes to the grave every Sunday if she can, when there's no snow. She just does it, she says. We cross the harbour over into the town of Pictou where they lived for four and half years. Past Hector Garage, Hector Building

Supplies. The Hector brought in Scottish settlers two hundred and some odd years ago, she tells me. Hector is a big name here. Pictou is a few streets paralleling the harbour, very picturesque, and old: 1767 at least. I wonder if that was a long time ago. Thick double-storeyed stone buildings squat here and there along the main thoroughfare—relics of another age bearing little plaques declaring their historicity. Up on the hill aging clapboard mansions stare out toward the harbour: widow's walks and high narrow windows, verandahs and pointed turrets carved in gingerbread, and enormous back ends built out in a jumble like piled wooden blocks.

The manse in Pictou is as big as the one in Stellarton, and Don's mother says it was just as cold in winter. A tang of distant paper mill hangs in the air. Tucked into the hillside in the centre of town a tiny triangular park slopes down toward its apex near the harbour: green grass, and a little round bandstand at the bottom. I recognize it as the park in one of Don's stories. "Don loved it here in Pictou," his mother says, "but he loved Glace Bay the most. In Glace Bay the explosions were terrible, you know. We had mass funerals. I remember one day when Don was eight years old: twenty-one men killed in one afternoon. We buried them in groups."

Don's mother is uncomfortable because she can't invite me to stay at her place. But I've got a motel room just so she won't feel obliged that way. And she's having dinner with friends tonight, something arranged long ago, and I'd planned to be on my own anyway, to walk around a while. We sit in the car for a few minutes while she explains the layout of the town. We're on Front Street. The Peter Pan is over to the right and then up. "So it's Marsh Street you'll be remembering," she says. "Don't forget that and you won't get lost." Marsh Street, I say to myself, bog. She tells me where to look for restaurants, warns me not to eat dinner in the Peter Pan. We're holding hands in the front seat of her little red car.

When I get out of the car it's a Sunday night in Nostrum. Walk to one end of the street and then back past the silent banks, the hardware store, the milliner's—all the shuttered shops. Rival taxi companies named for Jim and Cliff: which one brought me here? I can't remember. No one else walks: I am the lone pedestrian. A single light bulb burns in a corner grocery where the proprietor lurks in the half-dark. I step inside and ask him about restaurants and he explains that he never goes out for dinner. I walk on through the gathering dusk, cross Pleasant Street, then pause at Temperance to take in the prospect: silent houses sombre among the trees, vacant looking, no lights on in any of them; and then the blasted acreage of a deserted shopping mall. Wind scours the asphalt. It's beginning to spit rain and my shoelaces have come undone. I stoop down to tie them and hear myself say there's nothing here: find the Peter Pan and eat dinner there, it won't matter. Into the wind then, back along the silent streets and up, toward the motel, along mnemonic Marsh. The downpour hits half a mile from shelter. Hunch up and push. At the corner people are getting out of cars and going into a church; maple trees lean over the sidewalk to keep the rain away from them. All the light has gone from the sky and I reach the motel in the black of night. The motel room is a concrete bunker painted hospital green. I turn on the lamps and strip off my shirt and pants and towel off. Then I sit on the bed for a few minutes and wait.

Speech is flattened out and fast in this part of Nova Scotia; people talk without bringing their lips together, in a kind of burble. The waitress speaks to me and her sentences sound like one long word: "Sure you don wan another beer? You're welcome to it, specially with the bars all closed. Go ahead 'n stay." She's very kind. The meal was tinned carrots and beans, charred bits of fish, brittle fried shrimp and stale buns. I linger over coffee and beer, waiting out a Sunday in Nostrum. Back in the room, the TV next door is so loud I can hear the voice of the man on the shopping channel praising the cubic zirconium ring: folks, you've still got two minutes, don't delay now, you'll just regret it later. The empty singsong rings in the hollow bricks. Sleep, when it comes, comes suddenly.

But I am awake as suddenly as it comes: belly-tight and breath-less—something frightens me. Again and again I sleep, I wake.

Nova Scotia seems to be precisely what I have imagined it to be: a low, windswept place of shoreline and black Atlantic; quaint gabled houses, fish boats and coal mines and high-steepled wooden churches. History covers the surface of this place, eclipsing the future, concealing the present. What happens here? The people look ordinary, like one's grandparents ought to have looked, plain in dress and manner, simple in speech. A computer shop boldly proclaims itself FUTURE WORLD, but inside there are no customers: the future has been staked out by the shopping malls at the edge of town, busy fluorescent places, grim and up to date, unmemoried and innocent of time.

Don's mother's name is Viola and she tells me to call her Vi, which is how she is known to her friends. Her sister's name is Mildred. Vi is seventy-four and Mildred is nine years older. Mildred is unwell and Vi is looking after her. By noon I'm checked out of the Peter Pan and I've got my stuff slung into the back seat of the Ford so Vi can take me back to her place for lunch. Mildred is resting in the easy chair when we get in, and she gets up to shake my hand. Mildred looks even more like Don than Vi does. Her dark eyes are big, magnified by the lenses in her spectacles. She's shorter than Vi and her hair is dusky blue and she speaks in little bursts, with a catch in her throat almost like a stutter. While Vi sets up the dining table Mildred shows me a photograph of three children sitting on a step. "Can you recognize Don?" she says. "He's the one in the middle. Aged five. The others are my own. They were all good friends." In this one Don looks like his father. "Yes," says Vi, "he took after his father until he was a teenager. Then he began to look like my side of the family. It was a surprise to us all." We sit down to cold ham, tomatoes and cucumbers, potato salad, garlic bread, relish, tea, salt and pepper. The tomato slices are thick and sweet: they're from the garden in the back yard. Vi gets up and brings in two whole tomatoes from the kitchen. "Here's what we're talking about," she says and holds them out to me. Mildred says: "A good pound or close to it, three-quarters at least." We're eating from china plates and using silverware. There are two forks by each plate and a butter knife on the butter dish. The cukes are from the garden too, and Vi made the relish. Vi insists that we eat everything. I spread the relish on the bread, the ham, the potato salad. She's up and down the whole time, getting more tea, more ham, more potato salad. She reaches over the table for Mildred's cup. "We don't stand on ceremony here," she says. "You just help yourself." Mildred looks over at me and says: "I must say that I feel like I know you. All those years we heard about you, Don's trips home. He'd come and see me in Halifax. He was full of stories about you, about all of you." My body feels too big for this intimate space; I am enormous between these tiny sisters. There's cake and ice cream for dessert, more tea. Vi apologizes for the tea, which she says is not strong enough. "Do you like coffee?" says Mildred. "Don loved his coffee." I roll a cigarette and Vi urges us onto the sofa, the easy chair: it's more comfortable that way, she says, we can relax and talk.

Weather is fickle in the east, much more dramatic than weather on the west coast. "Out there it's so warm, though, isn't it?" Mildred says. She's never been out west and she supposes now that she never will be—that's one regret she has, not travelling more while she was young. Vi remembers Don writing years ago that he had bought an umbrella in Vancouver, something you would never do in Nova Scotia. "But everyone out there had umbrellas, he said; there was no stigma attached." When the snow comes Vi leaves her car in the garage. The snow makes her too nervous to drive. In fact, Don was going to come home that last winter, but she'd suggested he put it off until spring, thinking about the snow. She regrets that now and says there's no point of course but she can't help it.

"Don was a happy boy," Mildred says, "wouldn't you say, Vi? Remember how much he loved Glace Bay. He wouldn't let you say a bad thing about Glace Bay, which is a filthy place, you know, very dirty. All that smoke. And the smell, remember that, Vi—that day in the car?" Vi says, "Oh, we had to laugh. I was telling Mildred about the fish plant—Don was in the back seat—the smell of that place, when the wind turned: it was a terrible smell, putrid. It made you sick. Well, Don became quite indignant. He said it was a fine smell, a good smell, and Glace Bay was a wonderful clean place. We had to laugh at him. I never cared for Glace Bay, really." Mildred says: "It was a filthy place. But Don wouldn't let you say a bad word." From time to time I look up at the pictures on the piano, then back at the open faces of these women who are so easy with me. Mildred advises me to quit smoking. Vi offers to make more tea. Soon I am no longer awkward, and we are all talking about the weather, about Don and the past, about politics, local dialects (here in Pictou County you'll hear them say *after*: I'm after having a cup of coffee. In Cape Breton they use *right*: I'm right tired—and they say *oi* instead of *i*: so it's Oi'm roight tired. Over in Yarmouth they drop the r, like Americans. Even Vi says cyahr for car) and then more about the weather, about relatives living and dead, about travelling on buses, trains and airplanes. The Greyhound depot is forty miles away, in Truro, and Vi has promised to to drive me there in time to get the bus for Wolfville, which is where Don went to college before moving out to the coast. When it's time to go I use the washroom and Vi closes the hall door behind me for extra privacy. Back in the little hallway I duck my head into Don's bedroom, which is Mildred's room now, and the room is filled with a red light from the afternoon sun burning in through maroon curtains. We say goodbye to Mildred at the front door and set out one last time in the Ford.

Vi knows the route well. She's cautious on the on-ramp and we stay in the right lane at a steady fifty miles an hour. She says she could drive it in her sleep, all those years taking Don into Truro for the bus to Wolfville, and then later the train out to Vancouver. I remember a line from one of Don's journals—Truro is a station on the road to night—and think of going to the grave again, but don't suggest it. Vi asks about Don's friends in the west, naming each one, and I fill her in with generalities. There's the question of Don's manuscripts too, so we discuss that for a while. "Don hid things from people, you know," she said. "He didn't want anyone to know he wasn't well. He didn't want me to worry about him. It was important to him to be on his own, I suppose, independent." I look out the window as we talk. Truro sits in a valley, a shallow trough along a river. We pass the train station, make our way through tree-lined avenues, past wooden mansions, Historic Sites and a Dairy Queen and then onto the asphalt apron in front of the depot. Vi waits in the car while I go in to confirm the bus. When I return I can feel the ticket bright yellow in my hand.

Vi gets out and looks up into my face. There are tears in her eyes and she holds onto my hand. "This is hard for me," she says, and we embrace once, twice, three times. From the door to the depot I turn and wave, and wave again from inside. She gets the Ford backed out and turned around. She waves one more time.

ICE AND FIRE

KADLUNA

A couple of years ago I received my first postcard from Pangnirtung, and I was excited to get it. Pangnirtung is a hamlet of about nine hundred people a few miles south of the Arctic Circle, at the north end of Cumberland Sound on Baffin Island, and I was born there fifty-one years ago. On one side of the card was a colour photograph of a dogsled scene with *Canadian Arctic* inscribed across a blue sky; on the other side was a message handwritten in Inuktitut syllabics, so I had no idea what it said, but after some study with a syllabics dictionary I found the three syllables of my own name as pronounced in Inuktitut: ᕐ ᐱ ᕕ . The signature was printed out in English: *Etooangat Aksayook*, the man I knew as *Eetowanga*, the man who looked after my parents and took my father out by dogsled to visit the winter camps. When he wrote the message on the postcard he would have been ninety-three years old.

When I visited Pangnirtung in the 1980s, Eetowanga gave me daily lessons in Inuktitut. He was very good at this, perhaps because he had never learned English but instead perfected ways of teaching outsiders to speak a version of his own language. My parents were reasonably fluent in Inuktitut, which, when my family moved south early in my childhood, became their secret language at home. As I tried to absorb a rudimentary vocabulary from Eetowanga, I felt the terrific frustration of being able to speak only a kind of baby talk. Only the very old people in the village could understand me; they too were familiar with the primitive speech of the adult outsider. In my notes from that time I find some of the stories that Eetowanga told during these lessons. How did I understand them? When he was young he fell between his komatik and his dogs as they surged down a slope of broken ice, and one of the runners crushed his hand and smashed over the back of his head. He put his hand in mine so I could feel the misshapen bone, and there was a bit missing from one of his fingers. Then he pulled my hand up to the back of his skull so I could feel the indentation in the bone. He told me that when his father, who I gathered was a great hunter, first encountered tea and tobacco and a clock, he threw them into the sea because they were useless. Eetowanga told me stories about my father, who had been very young, and the older doctors who had preceded him. One afternoon I swatted a fly and managed to make a sentence of my own: *I, a hunter of flies*, I meant it to mean (in my notes I find *nivingaksilpoong*), and Eetowanga understood me although no one else did. He told funny stories of *kadluna*, the white men who made mistakes, like the American who caught a hook just below his left eye while trying to land a fish at a place called Clearwater. Eetowanga owned a three-wheel Honda motorcycle with fat tires and I hung onto his tiny waist as he wheeled me through the village. He was as old as the century. In my father's journal of thirty-five years earlier, I had read of Eetowanga telling my father that in a dream his first wife had appeared to tell him that he would live a long life and would die in the white man's hospital. There was no way I could tell him that I had heard this story, and I felt an uneasiness simply in knowing it.

During my visit Eetowanga's daughter Rosie, who had tended me when I was a baby, and her husband Pauloosie took me with their two kids fishing in their small cabin cruiser with twin seventy-fives on the back. We shot out over the reef and down to the mouth of the fiord into the astonishing blue ocean ringed by glittering white shore ice that lay melting in the sun. We anchored on an icepan that looped out from the shore and I could see the salmon circling in the deep pool. I had the wrong boots on, with hard soles, and kept working my heels down into the soft ice as I cast into the pool with Pauloosie's big rod. When the strike came I could feel my feet slipping as I leaned back and the fish leapt into the air and the kids (who had been silent until now) started yelling and talking and running along beside me. I kept the rod tip up because I remembered reading in a book that that's what you did, and when the fish went down I scrambled backwards from the water's edge. I felt wholly incompetent. But the kids were still chattering and I realized that the fish was still hooked so I kept working the reel and felt myself again sliding down toward the water as the adrenalin pumped ridiculously through my awkward flailing body. The fish came up again and went back down and still I had not fallen in. I could hear the kids and I couldn't understand what they were saying, but then I heard two words I knew, recurring in their high-pitched voices: *ilkaloo, ilkaloo: fish*, I said to myself, that's *fish;* and then *kadluna, kadluna: me*—the *kadluna* was me. I felt a shock run through me: until this moment, *kadluna* had been merely an expression, a reference to some species of other person. But now in a moment I was found out, revealed to be that which I had not known myself to be. *Ilkaloo?* I called out, *ilkaloo-juak!* Not *just* a fish, I meant to say: but a big fish, a very big fish! I dug in my heels and worked the rod back into the air. This was my release into foreignness.

SUMMER HOUSE

We had been at the family reunion only a few minutes when I heard someone say, "Are you from Moses or from Aaron?" We were in the summer house in the middle of a community park twenty miles out of Vancouver. It was a hot summer day, but it was cool in the summer house, which lay in the shadow of enormous evergreen trees beyond which could be glimpsed a ball field where a softball game was underway. The park was filled with people, old, young and middle-aged, strolling through the trees, picnicking at park benches and sitting in the bleachers behind the backstop. One side of the summer house was given over to card tables for the cribbage players, older people wearing baseball caps and cotton prints and light windbreakers; on the other side a small crowd had gathered around a photocopier, from the back of which hung an orange extension cord that ran down the steps and out onto the ground across the park to a distant powerhouse. The photocopier was the real heart of the reunion: the people standing around it had with them copies of old letters, deeds, birth records, obituaries, bills of sale, newspaper clippings—all the stuff of genealogy—which the young woman operating the machine patiently copied for them, and which they exchanged with the alacrity of bargainers at a swap meet.

This was the reunion of the family Eames, also spelt Emes or Ames, a line that descended through my mother's mother, and about whom I had known nothing until this moment in the summer house, when my mother, who had invited me to attend, informed me that all of the people in the park, including the cribbage players and the people playing baseball, were relatives of mine. I was surprised that a secret of such great size (there must have been two hundred people in the park) could have been kept from me for more than forty years, and I felt a childish resentment at the prospect of having to admit all these new relations into my world. This was the first assembly of the Eameses to occur west of the Rockies, and my mother, whose mother's maiden name had been unknown to me until today, assured me that had such a reunion taken place when I was younger she would have brought me along that much earlier.

I surveyed the park full of strangers who had been transformed in a moment into family, and tried to remember my mother's mother, a fierce woman whom I had met only a few times in childhood, and whose presence had put me in mind of Queen Victoria. I knew nothing of my grandmother's forebears, and I had never asked (as my mother reminded me when I suggested that she had been keeping a secret) about where any of my grandparents had come from. The past that I carried within me began with my parents and ended with their parents; anything older than that lay obscured in a mist that I associated with an obsolete England similar to the one described by Charles Dickens in *Bleak House*. I had never, except in the most abstract way, considered my life to be a consequence of history. But now I was no longer alone and first in my world; indeed, I was now linked irrevocably to a galaxy of strangers whose habit it was to gather in public parks in order to exchange personal information.

Now I approached the family tree, a composite document that covered part of a wall in the summer house. A number of my relatives were gathered in front of it, tracing portions of it with their fingers. I had to study it for some time before it began to make sense; then I found my grandmother's name near the bottom of the document and off to one side, and on another sheet attached to that one, my mother's name and then my own name, and the names of my brother and sisters. It was then a matter of tracing connections back to the centre of the document and up toward the ceiling. Here I found Moses and Aaron Emes, twins born a hundred and sixty-five years ago; each of them had ten children (one of Aaron's children was the father of my grandmother)—and above them more branches moving back through the eighteenth century and the American Revolution to the Indian Wars in New England in the seventeenth century until, at the top of the tree near the ceiling of summer house, inscribed with a broad-nib pen, the name of the first Eames ancestor: Thomas, age twelve, Massachusetts, 1634, a mere fourteen years after the first voyage of the *Mayflower*. Of Thomas's ancestors, nothing but a summary remark written next to his name: "from the west of England."

So began my history among the Puritans of Massachusetts, usurpers of an ancient world, a people that I had never admired. I stood back for a moment to contemplate the past as outlined on the summer house wall, and felt the screen of my anonymity leaving me forever: nothing had changed, but now everything was different. I was surrounded by the descendants of Thomas, Aaron, Moses, and I was one of them, a picnicker in a public park, a consequence of history. I went over to the copy machine and joined the crowd exchanging documents, and the young woman operating the machine, whom I addressed as Cousin, began making extra copies for me.

Later, in the bundle of paper that I took home from the park, I found a copy of a letter written in 1833 by a man named Daniel Gill, whom I calculate on the family tree to be one of my great-great-great-grandfathers; he writes from Hadley, New York, to his son Jacob at Lake Simcoe in Canada, to whom he confesses that he deserted the British Army forty-five years earlier, and is still under sentence of death should he return to Canada to visit his son. He doesn't say why he waited nearly half a century to tell the story.

Other notes in my bundle identify Daniel Gill as a foot soldier who served under Benedict Arnold against the American rebels in 1781 and deserted in 1787 in New Brunswick; his son Jacob went to Canada in 1812 at age sixteen; they never saw each other again. What drew Jacob to Canada when the U.S.A. and Canada were at war? Another grandfather at three removes I find fighting for the revolutionary army, and thirty years later his son Silas in Canada is fighting for the British in the war against the Americans; in 1837 Silas joins in the action against the Canadian rebels of William Lyon Mackenzie at Montgomery's Tavern, along with thirty-five other men from his neighbourhood, one of whom is identified in a single reference as a "Mr. Osborne."

As I followed these divisions of the family tree across wars of conquest and revolution, I could feel the past entering my life as something new to be learned rather than something old to be remembered. Also in my bundle was a sheaf of papers entitled "The Framingham Massacre," which is an account of the deaths of the second wife of the original Thomas (my grandparent at eight or nine removes), and four of their nine children when their farm was attacked by warriors of the Wampanoag Nation during the war known in history books as "King Phillip's War." I knew the history of this war, which was the last and most devastating of the wars between the New England colonists and the Native inhabitants, and I remembered reading of the Framingham Massacre years ago, but I was moved to pay more attention to the story when it came to me tangled in personal relations. Thomas's second wife's name was Mary and she died while pouring boiling soap over the attackers; the children who survived were all taken captive; two of them escaped and two or three were taken into Canada, a Catholic country, and sold to Canadians. Of these last, at least one, and possibly, two, chose not to return to New England when it became possible to do so, having received, in the words of a family narrator writing in 1847, "very kind usage from the French inhabitants."

ICE AND FIRE

In November 1995, my father, who was seventy years old, flew from Vancouver to Ottawa to see his old mentor Eetowanga Aksayook of Pangnirtung, Baffin Island, who was ninety- four years old and would be in Ottawa to receive the Order of Canada from the Governor General. In the snapshot my father is taller than Eetowanga by more than a head, but they both have the faces of old men, and I can see that my father's eyes have narrowed over the years into a permanent squint nearly as intense as Eetowanga's.

My father's plane had been forced by a blizzard to land in Montreal and then he had to backtrack to Ottawa through the blizzard on a Greyhound bus. This gave my father the satisfaction of having to overcome obstacles in order to be with the man who fifty years ago had shown him how to build a snowhouse on a frozen sea. A few weeks before leaving Vancouver, my father got out the Inuktitut dictionary and grammar that he had made under Eetowanga's instruction so many years ago. He needed to brush up on the language. Eetowanga, who had worked with three generations of doctors from the south, had never found it necessary to learn English. This was part of his genius.

The trip to Ottawa was the first time Eetowanga had ever been south of Baffin Island. He flew from Pangnirtung on Cumberland Sound to Iqaluit on Frobisher Bay with his grandson Billy, and then they got the flight out over Hudson Strait and down to Ottawa. His daughter Lucy had flown out a few days early to confirm the hotel and arrange for the tuxedo.

My parents went to Pangnirtung in 1946, on a ship that took a month to make its way around Baffin Island and into Cumberland Sound. My mother was twenty-one and my father was twenty-three. In the photographs they look completely brand new. Eetowanga was there in the small boat to greet them and bring them ashore. They looked like children to him, he told me many years later. It was his job to keep them alive. My father had been designated coroner and justice of the peace, as well as settlement doctor, by the government of William Lyon Mackenzie King. This was during the last phase of the colonialist project in North America, although neither my parents nor Eetowanga thought of it that way then. In the photographs can be seen a scattering of permanent buildings along the foreshore—Hudson's Bay Company post, missionary's house, police station, hospital, doctor's house; and then on closer scrutiny, an array of smaller, impermanent dwellings that seem, in black and white, to blend with the rolling tundra. These were the homes of the permanent population, the people who called themselves human beings in a language that neither of my parents had ever heard before. Eetowanga began teaching them that language on their first day ashore.

When Eetowanga was still a young man, his wife became ill and he took her to the hospital at Pangnirtung. Soon he was working for the hospital, and in the great paratyphoid epidemic of the late thirties, he saved the lives of many people in Cumberland Sound, working tirelessly over many days and nights carrying the sick from their camps in to the hospital. This was one of the things he was known for around Cumberland Sound, where he earned great respect as hunter and trapper, guide and protector. Late into his seventies he was still taking visitors onto the land and the sea, a territory of five thousand square miles of water and ice, tundra and mountain, that was to him no territory at all, but the place where he lived.

I asked my father how it was that Eetowanga could manage without English and my father waited a moment and said: He always seemed to know my mind, he taught me everything the same way he taught his children. A page in my father's journal bears a single notation: "Explanation of thunder and lightning from Eetowanga: He begins by urinating. Then he strikes flint for fire. Then he rubs violently on a piece of stiff seal skin, in order to soften it." Another page carries the title "Water Substitutes in the Arctic" followed by short instructions, two of which are: "If you are to be away from camp, eat a lot of fat while on the trail. In this way you will be less thirsty," and "If there is glacier ice, make a hole in it big enough for your head, and build a fire in the hole with oil or fat, using a piece of cloth for a wick. After a few minutes, blow aside the fat and soot, and drink the water."

In his hotel room in Ottawa, Eetowanga told Lucy and Billy the story of my father and the parka. They had made camp far out on the ice of Kingnait Fiord and my father, worried about how he would get his clothes on in the morning in the tiny space of the snow house, devised the plan of assembling his two parkas (the inside one a duffel parka and the outside a fur parka) beforehand by inserting the inside one into the outside one. Then, in underwear, trousers and boots, he would rush out of the snowhouse and drop the parka set over his head before freezing to death in the gale-force wind. (The temperature was forty below zero.) When the moment came, Eetowanga was outside with the dogs, waiting. My father rolled out of the igloo, leapt to his feet, dropped the double parkas over his head and thrust his arms into the sleeves. It was a smooth operation, but for one detail: the inside parka was backwards to the outside one; the inner hood fell onto my father's face, perfectly protecting him from the wind but blinding him at the same time by freezing instantly to his face. As he scrambled to

get the parkas off and reassembled, my father could feel his hands
freezing, but then Eetowanga was there laughing and rubbing his
hands and helping him work the stiff garments back onto his body.
There was nothing to worry about, he said; as far as he knew no
one had ever died from the cold while putting on a parka. This was
an important thing for me to know at the time, my father said,
when he told me the story only a few years ago.

When Eetowanga was a child, the European whalers were still
operating in Cumberland Sound. This was before World War
One. In the stories of Eetowanga's childhood which my father
transcribed into his journals, the past can be heard as two different
stories: one, familiar to me, begins in Europe and is often told as
the discovery of the north; the other is much more elusive, and
begins entirely elsewhere, in a place outside of my imagination. In
this direction lie the stories of Eetowanga's ancestors, beginning
with his father, a man Eetowanga described to my parents with a
word that might be translated as *irascible*. Eetowanga's father was
known in his day as a great walker, a strong man whose feet
adhered to the ground. During a heavy famine at Padle camp,
when the last of the dogs had been eaten, a woman respected for
her dreams reported a dream which indicated that Eetowanga's
father might be able to save the camp by walking to Kekerten, an
island about a hundred miles away over rough ice, which he would
have to do in three days if no one was to die. At Kekerten he would
find supplies and dogs with which to carry them back. This was
an impossible thing to do, but Eetowanga's father set out immedi-
ately to do it. On the third day the woman respected for her dreams
reported that Eetowanga's father had succeeded and that he would
be arriving the next day with food and supplies. This news enraged
the husband of the dreaming woman (possibly he was jealous of
Eetowanga's father). The husband then set out for Kekerten him-
self, and he was never seen again. The next day Eetowanga's father
appeared in the camp with a komatik loaded with food and

ammunition, and all but the husband of the woman respected for her dreams were saved.

Sometime in 1947, which is the year I was born, Eetowanga told my father that people around Pangnirtung had been rethinking a very old question: which was stronger, the cold or the heat? Traditional opinion had held the two to be in equilibrium, but recently people had begun to think in other ways and now some were saying that the cold was stronger because people could be killed by it, whereas the sun had never been known to kill anyone. This was my father's introduction to the mutability of the world of human beings.

Eetowanga had no desire to go looking around Ottawa, but preferred instead to hang around the Chateau Laurier with his relatives and with my father, taking it easy and talking about the past. This was fine with my father, who had never hung around in a hotel before in his life. The night of the ceremony my father remained in the hotel as he had been told that there was no room in the Governor General's house for onlookers. He went down to the lobby with Eetowanga and when they saw that a thick icy rain was falling, Eetowanga returned to his room to get something to put on his head. When he got back to the lobby he was wearing a Montreal Canadiens cap. Here then was my father's mentor, setting off from the steps of the Chateau Laurier to receive the Order of Canada: a short, handsome man with very narrow eyes, in tuxedo, baseball cap and running shoes, a man who referred to himself as *Inutuinak*—a word my father's dictionary translates as "merely a human being."

Eetowanga Aksayook died in Pangnirtung in January 1996. He is remembered in the north and in the south.

OPEN THE DOOR

O lift me up and carry me
In a throne down to the sea
I will show you all your kings
Where the wave doth loudly sing.
Place the crown upon my head
Put the sceptre in my hand
It will be done as you have said
I'll drive the sea back from the land

—from "Song For Canute,"
by Jon Furberg

My friend Jon Furberg died a week before Christmas, late in the morning, wearing his favourite shirt, the white one with the big sleeves, in his wife's arms, at home in his own bed. He was in pain and deteriorating rapidly with cancer. He had to have help to get the shirt on, and to sit up in the bed. I am told that he asked to be alone with R, his spiritual advisor; when they were alone he said to R, please close the door—when you think it appropriate, open it again. They spoke together for some minutes, and then Jon was silent and R said: do you want to lie down now? R opened the door and some minutes later Jon stopped breathing.

Late in the afternoon, when I learned that Jon was dead, I felt the breath leave my body. I put down the phone and looked over to the front of the office, where a few weeks ago Jon had been standing and talking to us. I had not expected him then, nor had I heard him come in; he seemed merely to have materialized after a long absence. I was in another room; I heard his voice and went eagerly to see him, but for a moment couldn't find him: in his place was a tall man with no hair. We were both very shy. In the coffee bar I said that I was learning to live without something—I can't remember what—and he took my hand in both of his big ones. Yes, yes, he said, and I wanted then to begin remembering that moment. A week later I went to see him and he said all that we are now is in who we were then, when we published books together, when we wrote songs. He said: I want to know what that means. He was speaking entirely in the present.

But many days passed after Jon died before I put the old tape into the machine in my room, so that I might once again hear him singing his songs, especially the song for Canute, the English king who promised to turn back the sea.

O set me down at the edge of the sea
And I will try to comfort thee
Pick me up like a fallen tree
Leave me lying in the sand.

(Song for Canute)

1966

When I was eighteen he was twenty-one. We met at a wild beer-drinking party in the summer. He was reciting his own poetry written in the manner of Dylan Thomas and I played "House of the Rising Sun" on the guitar in the manner of Bob Dylan. He was a big tall man with tremendously bushy hair and a cherubic face. Everything about him made me want to outdo myself.

1972

The drawings are straight black and white on big foot-and-a-half by two-foot pieces of repro paper, a dozen heavy sheets rolled up for so long that now when I spread them on the table their corners recoil and wrap themselves over my fingers.

On each sheet, two or three sketches depict a number of hairy men in a diversity of postures, their outlines rendered in a quick, nearly weightless line that threatens to burst out into the white perimeter. The artist has enlarged the hands of his subjects, made them thick with lumpy fingers wrapped around beer bottles, cigarettes, pencils, pens. There are five men in the drawings. Four of them wear their shirttails outside their pants. They are all engaged in some kind of work and carry intense expressions in their faces, hilarious perhaps, or demonic.

In one drawing I am leaning over a metal box. I wear an undershirt and hold a bottle of beer in my hand. In another my brother Tom is sketching Furberg at a typesetting keyboard. Furberg has huge spatulate fingers: they are the real subject of this drawing. He plunges them down into the keys two at a time; at his left elbow floats a bottle of beer. Images of Furberg dominate the drawings: his curly hair and his big hands recur on each sheet.

We are preparing Jon's first book of poetry for the printing press and Tom is drawing us as we work. Tom sits behind a desk across the room. He is wearing a tee shirt. In his right hand the felt pen moves over the page, but he doesn't look at it; he looks only at us. Fraser sits beside him, poring over galleys. Fraser is the proof-reader; he wears a chequered short-sleeved shirt with a button-down collar. Fraser is the one with his shirttail tucked in. It is summer and it hasn't rained for weeks. We are hot and we sweat as we work, but we persist until the beer supply is exhausted. Then at ten or eleven we collect the empties and stash them in the back room and clean up the shop, which has been loaned to us for this work.

Before leaving, we load the magnetic tape into the Output Device and print out what we've done. We gather around the machine and I tell Fraser (in this sketch, the tiny bearded man standing directly in front) which key to hit. Gingerly he extends a hand, index finger outstretched. The tape hums, and the machine erupts into a staccato hammering as the print head begins to trip along the platen. We watch the metal ball move back and forth, beating lines of poetry into the chalky paper, and Fraser begins to read the words aloud to its machine-gun rhythm. Now-the-fit-moves-again—weaving-fish-and-men-urging-words; and we join him: from-what-minds-mouth-to-sound-the-whale-miclan-hwala, lifting our voices in a metrical cacophony.

At the front of the office, on the other side of the big window, people waiting for the bus peer in at us; they approach the glass but don't touch it: they look in at five hairy men who have their arms on each other's shoulders, five men who are looking down at something and laughing, and making an incomprehensible noise.

These drawings have been lying in a trunk for many years. They have a musty smell about them, like a box of old photographs. But unlike photographs, they are most evidently *renderings*—idiosyncratic in detail and contour—and they seem, in their insistence upon themselves as made things, to create their own time, rather than to preserve or even to reflect some other one.

But of course—to render is also to *give back*—and, implicitly, to make a rendezvous.

1976

Jon brought a soil-testing kit out to where I was trying to make a garden. He wanted me to get it right, with the little test tubes and coloured powders. We messed around for a couple of hours making the tests before deciding the garden needed a dose of lime. Then we drove off to get the lime and some beer, and late in the afternoon under a lowering sun we began to scatter the white powder over the ground. A light breeze had come up and the lime dust drifted in clouds in the bright palpitating air and we felt an eerie sensation looking into it: so must the Romans have felt scattering salt over the burnt soil of Carthage, we thought, and then we thought of the other, equally terrible sowing of lime into the mass graves of Europe. Jon had been working for six years on the poems that would make up *Anhaga*, and four more years would pass before he finished it. *Pray for hardship*, one of those poems begins: *all earth's a common mound.* We both liked to watch Hollywood Bible epics, for those echoes of transcendence that can only be felt when one is properly attuned to them, late at night in front of the television set. *Barabbas* was my favourite; *The Robe* was his.

1983

He had resolved to publish poems only after he had worked on them for ten years. From this we derived the notion, never realized, of a ten-year-poetry-writing competition: register now, come back in ten years with your poem (and don't bother us in the meantime). But before *Anhaga* was complete, Jon found himself with another small book that had taken only a couple of years to write. This was *Prepositions for Remembrance Day*, and we published it despite the ten-year rule. We had discovered new significance in Remembrance Day after reading Paul Fussell's book *The Great War and Modern Memory*, and taken to wearing poppies on the 11th of November.

THUMB

Together we built the side porch and the two flights of stairs and the landing between them. We knew almost nothing of building but we knew how to read books, in this case two thick carpentry books that we kept by us at all times. It took us the whole summer, and of course we had to do everything twice, from setting concrete foundations to brushing stain onto the cedar balustrade. One day we were trying to force a four-by-four into position and Jon was whacking the end of it with the big hammer and I was holding it steady with my face very close to the end of the board. It was an awkward position and we were perched high on the landing, on top of each other. Again and again the hammer swept past my head and thwacked on the timber-end and I could feel the post move in my hands. Then I saw the thumb of Jon's left hand slip into range and before I could speak, it exploded under the hammer head with an astonishingly dull thunk. Somehow we got down onto the ground and I pulled Jon's hand out away from his side to look at it. The end of his thumb was a ruined mess; bits of cartilage and not much blood, and white stuff leaking out around the edges. Jon said, My God, you know what that is? He was whispering. That's *fatty tissue*, he said. And then he fainted. He was out for only a few seconds but I felt his whole weight upon me in that time as I strove to hold him up, and in my distress felt not his pain, but some direct equivalent of it: an urgent wish to draw it from him, to absorb it into my body as I clung to him, stumbling, holding him up against sheer gravity.

1992

The chemotherapy worked in a three-week cycle. The first week was incapacitating, the second slightly better, and in the third he felt himself back in the world. So I was surprised to see him in what I calculated to be still a second week when he showed up at the publishing party in late November. He was wearing a floppy cap to keep his head warm, and a long overcoat. We talked and I saw him talking to other people. For some time he remained standing

197

at the back of the room, and then when I looked up he was no longer there.

> And tell the sky to bring for me
> A wind that blows for all of thee
> And spread the the cloud along the sea
> And send the wave down over me
> and send the wave
> down over me
>
> *(Song for Canute)*

FALL

The night of the day that Jon died I put off sleep as long as possible, afraid of what I might find there. Instead I sat in the front room of the apartment and stared out the window at the first snowfall of the year, a thing that Jon would never see. There was still so much to have been better done, or undone; and then words too—words better to have been said, or unsaid. The falling snow held me in a trance; it was too soon to begin mourning.

In the dream I knew immediately that I was running late, but there remained nevertheless things that had to be done before leaving town: the familiar burdens of preparation and arrangement were upon me. I recall driving into the country to rendezvous with old friends, none of whom were there. But on returning I saw Jon, who was standing on the corner with no hair, and his baldness seemed to put an *imprimatur* on things. By a wonderful coincidence he had booked himself on the same flight that I had, so without further discussion we fell into an arrangement requiring only that we get to the airport together, and things began to accelerate while nothing appeared to be happening any more quickly. Eventually I was packing a suitcase and everything seemed to be working out when I found Jon by agreement in a crowded mall in the centre of the city. An enormous crowd of people were streaming through corridors and we were swept into them as into a vortex—*vortex*, I said to myself, right then, this is a vortex; Jon looked at me and smiled and I knew that he was reading my mind. But just then I didn't want him to know what I was thinking. We both had suitcases and he was wearing a trench coat. I looked at him again and strove to match my stride to his as we swept up and around the spiral walkway, and eventually the crowd fell away and we were loping tirelessly upward, decelerating at every step but breathing steadily. We burst into open air, and all at once the ocean of the world lay at our feet, and I knew that we were irrevocably late for the flight, that we would never make it to the airport.

Now before us lay only the horizon, a distant watery meniscus; all was silence and blue light; behind us lay the confusion and the noise of details and crowded tunnels; I felt the tickets slip from my hand. I had begun to suspect that Jon was no longer alive, and now I was convinced of it. I turned to speak to him and he was no longer at my side. For a moment I thought he had deserted me and felt all my resolution sweep away. Only then did I see him: he was sitting on a rampart a short distance beneath me, closer to the ocean. He was naked and appeared to be looking out at the horizon; I could see the top of his bald head and the extent of his big shoulders: the whole enormous sadness of the world seemed to emanate from his body. And then the great distant yolk of ocean began to pulse up toward us, rising and surging, and the horizon with it, and I looked down at Jon who never looked up or back over his shoulder; certainly he didn't look back at me; and then he simply flung himself out from the land with his arms in front of him—rather sluggishly, it seemed to me—in an idle kind of belly-flop, and began falling into the ocean as lazily as the ocean was falling up toward him, toward me. But before colliding with the ocean he began to level out and to accelerate; and then he shot straight out over the ocean into the yellow horizon and disappeared forever from sight.

Now I was alone. The ocean had ceased pulsing and the horizon lay before me in its perfect concavity. I was confused, and worried that I might be violating the rules of dreaming. I looked out toward the distance into which Jon had accelerated and wondered whether I would ever be able to do that; and as suddenly knew that I would never know unless I jumped now; and so against all the laws of dreaming, I leapt, or let myself fall, from the solid place on which I had been standing, into the great ocean of the world.

I fell; I plummeted; I felt the breath leave my body. I would have hit the water, had not my body suddenly swept out onto the horizontal; that was when I saw the sun rushing toward me and I knew I had achieved acceleration, that I was speeding toward that point at which everything turns to light.